Permission to Put Yourself First

ALSO BY
<u>NANCY LEVIN</u>

<u>Books</u>

Worthy

Jump . . . And Your Life Will Appear

Writing for My Life

<u>Audio Programs</u>

Worthy

Jump . . . And Your Life Will Appear

All of the above are available at your local bookstore, or may be
ordered by visiting:

Hay House UK: www.hayhouse.co.uk
Hay House USA: www.hayhouse.com®
Hay House Australia: www.hayhouse.com.au
Hay House India: www.hayhouse.co.in

Permission to Put Yourself First

QUESTIONS, EXERCISES AND ADVICE TO TRANSFORM ALL YOUR RELATIONSHIPS

NANCY LEVIN

HAY HOUSE

Carlsbad, California • New York City
London • Sydney • New Delhi

Published in the United Kingdom by:
Hay House UK Ltd, The Sixth Floor, Watson House,
54 Baker Street, London W1U 7BU
Tel: +44 (0)20 3927 7290; Fax: +44 (0)20 3927 7291; www.hayhouse.co.uk

Published in the United States of America by:
Hay House Inc., PO Box 5100, Carlsbad, CA 92018-5100
Tel: (1) 760 431 7695 or (800) 654 5126
Fax: (1) 760 431 6948 or (800) 650 5115; www.hayhouse.com

Published in Australia by:
Hay House Australia Ltd, 18/36 Ralph St, Alexandria NSW 2015
Tel: (61) 2 9669 4299; Fax: (61) 2 9669 4144; www.hayhouse.com.au

Published in India by:
Hay House Publishers India, Muskaan Complex, Plot No.3, B-2,
Vasant Kunj, New Delhi 110 070
Tel: (91) 11 4176 1620; Fax: (91) 11 4176 1630; www.hayhouse.co.in

A catalogue record for this book is available from the British Library.

This title was previously published as *The New Relationship
Blueprint* (ISBN: 978-1-4019-5509-0)

Tradepaper ISBN: 978-1-78817-393-3
E-book ISBN: 978-1-4019-5844-2

Interior design: Nick C. Welch

Printed and bound by CPI Group (UK) Ltd, Croydon, CR0 4YY

for aaron
love 2.0

i used to
feel small
and sinking

so afraid of
being swallowed

today
i feel your heart
reeling me in
above waterline
to breathe again
with deep gratitude
knowing there is no one else
i'd want by my side
as we explore
the labyrinth of love

now
i remember
air is always available
in love with you

♥

Contents

Introduction

"You complete me."

Tom Cruise was on my TV screen saying that line to Renée Zellweger in the movie *Jerry Maguire*, causing women the world over to swoon.

But not me. "It's more like you *deplete* me," I mumbled to myself.

If you've read my book *Jump . . . And Your Life Will Appear*, you already know everything you need to know about my marriage. "Depleting" would be a very generous way to describe it, so it's no wonder I reacted this way to such romantic schmaltz on TV.

It took me years to stop thinking I needed a permission slip to be myself and do what I wanted. Years to discover that my life is my own and that I don't owe anything to anyone else. Years to get free from believing that the only way to get love is to buy it, by bending over backward with people-pleasing. Years to live life from my own inspiration, motivation, and agency—rather than in response or reaction to anyone or anything else.

Is it any wonder, then, that I even found myself feeling nauseated sitting at a dear friend's wedding? It was a wedding like at the end of every romantic movie, times about a billion. The gorgeous, joyous, and madly-in-love couple exchanged tender vows, pledging their hearts and souls to one another against a sunlit, waterfront backdrop. It was magnificent, and I'm sure most of the other women (and many of the men) were thinking, *If only this could be me.*

Yet, as I sat there watching the ceremony, all I could think was, *I* don't want *what they're having!* I just couldn't see anything positive or realistic in that kind of marital union.

A few weeks later, I told my sister as much. "I feel like I'm never going to say 'I love you' or hear those words from anyone else again. At least not in the way they said it at that wedding."

Truth be told, I believed I was 100 percent finished with romantic relationships. All I wanted was to be alone. Gloriously *alone.* I didn't want to live with anyone ever again. Living with someone meant taking another person's needs into account, and that was something I was simply not up for.

In the months and years that followed the end of my marriage, I dove into all kinds of personal growth work. I learned that I wasn't very good at taking care of my own needs first, so I focused a lot of my attention there. I learned how to love and accept myself, and how to follow my own desires. I investigated my shadow selves, learned who I was without a husband, and discovered that I don't have to mold myself into something I'm not in order to be loved and appreciated by others.

Singlehood suited me. It was truly wonderful to have no one to answer to. I could make my own decisions, free from the obligations of relationship. And best of all, I could work as much as I wanted to! For this workaholic, it was heaven. I had finally reached the place where I could say, "I'm free! Nothing triggers me anymore. I am woman— hear me roar!" I was officially D.O.N.E. with romance.

Or so I thought.

As it turned out, it didn't take long for a surprise to enter my life. His name was Aaron.

We were introduced by friends, although they weren't trying to fix us up. In fact, they didn't expect us to be a match at all. They knew a relationship with a new man was the last thing I was looking for, and we were such different people they never imagined us hitting it off. But there he was, and the attraction was undeniable. Before I could even fully process what was happening, we were together.

Suddenly, I discovered that rubbing up against another human being—literally or figuratively—causes all of that "I'm free! I am woman!" stuff to go flying right out the window. All of my old emotional issues had just been lying in wait, and I realized I'd been isolating myself in part to avoid them.

Here's one of the big lessons I learned: Each of us is the common denominator in all of our relationships, and we'll always draw others to us who will activate our deepest emotional issues. This is true in work, friendship, and family life, and it goes doubly if we're talking about intimate relationship. There's simply no way to prevent "our stuff" from following us around until we're ready to deal with it.

While my ex-husband and my current boyfriend, Aaron, are very different, there are ways in which they're frighteningly similar. And it's the ways they're similar that activate my "core wounds," which are my deepest hurts from childhood. For example, Aaron has abandonment issues, while I have suffocation issues. When it gets hard, I want space, and he wants more closeness . . . which triggers my need for *even more* alone time, which triggers his need for *even more* interaction. See how our wounds fit together in perfect . . . um . . . "harmony"?

Crazy enough, that's the nature of any healthy relationship. Which goes completely against everything we learn in the Disney-style fairy-tale version of relationship, where everything is supposed to be sunshine, butterflies, and sweet little songs all day long.

As you'll learn in the pages that follow, consistent harmony usually means there's a lot of churning going on under the surface. Why? Because our core wounds—and the limiting beliefs they have installed in our unconscious—*want* to be healed. That movement toward healing is a drive within us that can't be denied, and relationship is a perfect opportunity for that healing. After all, who holds up a mirror, reflecting our own wounds back to us, more fully than a primary partner? As I'll explain in greater detail, the qualities in ourselves that we've deemed bad or wrong—the "shadow selves" that we've disowned—usually show up as qualities in our intimate partners. In other words, what we refuse to see in ourselves is guaranteed to be called forth in those to whom we are closest. (You heard me: You can stop blaming your partner, because he or she is simply showing you the parts of yourself you don't want to see.)

Before you reach for the barf bag, let me assure you that there is good news here. Because it stirs the pot so effectively, intimate relationship can become a key teacher in our lives. It can actually become a spiritual practice, guiding us toward more awareness and freedom. In fact, mining our so-called "relationship issues" for the gold they contain is the basis of transforming your relationship from the inside-out, and creating the new relationship blueprint I'll set forth in this book.

A NEW RELATIONSHIP BLUEPRINT

My relationship with Aaron is about love, joy, sex, and all the other good stuff everyone wants. But it's also a way for each of us to learn more about our inner landscape and heal the hurt places within. Our relationship confronts us and challenges us to evolve—every single day. Sometimes it's messy, sometimes it's graceful, sometimes it's unskilled, and sometimes it's glorious. But the most important difference between my marriage and my relationship with Aaron is that there's an ongoing, conscious, collaborative conversation under way about our triggers and issues, as well as our hopes and dreams.

When I say "triggers," I'm talking about those reactive emotional responses that happen when we project our own shadow onto someone else. For example, I pride myself on being the least lazy person on the planet. In fact, for most of my life, I've judged laziness as a deadly sin. I can come up with a court-approved list of arguments to condemn anyone I believe is being lazy. So you can imagine that I'm easily triggered when I think someone else—especially my partner in life and love—is being lazy.

Aaron knows this trigger of mine . . . very well. He and I operate very differently in the world. I tend to be a "leap before I look" person, assuming I can figure out any obstacle in my path. Aaron, on the other hand, is a much more thoughtful decision maker. He weighs all the options, contemplates possible outcomes, and then takes small steps, rather than trying to make the whole thing happen in a single day. The result of this difference is that I can run circles around him productivity-wise. For longer than I'd like to admit, I've been triggered by what I saw as an overemphasis on enjoying his life. That trigger would send me reacting with overwork, as I labeled his thoughtfulness "lazy."

It has taken years for me to recognize that his thoughtful approach has as much value as my impulsive one, for very different reasons. I've also learned that I've long projected my own natural laziness onto other people, making them wrong for operating in the world differently than I do. But guess what? When I can show compassion toward the naturally lazy part of me, the trigger is diminished. When I can't show that compassion, I get angry or reject the person I've projected my laziness on.

Lucky for me, Aaron has been a willing participant in my self-discovery—and I in his. (He's got his own triggers and projections, some of which I will be sharing later in the book, with his gracious permission.) What's different from relationships I've had in the past is that we're both genuinely excited and interested in exploring who we are in relationship, why we behave the way we do, and what our emotional triggers can teach us about ourselves and one another. We're committed to having open, loving communication about it with each other. We're always *all in.*

This has been huge for me. It's the first relationship in which I've had that kind of openness and willingness to be present with each other, no matter what.

One of our goals is to find the meeting place between us—a place where neither of us has to abandon our true selves for the sake of the relationship. We've worked to build a relationship "container" that can hold the truth of each of us, that can hold our differences, and that can hold us where we need to be held the most. As a result, we've learned how to stay emotionally connected, even when we're embroiled in conflict.

So perhaps there's something else available in between "you complete me" and "you deplete me." Perhaps it could best be stated as "you complement me." The new relationship blueprint calls for two whole people to be in partnership with each other in a way that honors the totality of each individual.

That's the foundation of the book you're holding in your hands. The goal is to reframe the way you love. When you put yourself first, you won't lose yourself in the process.

These pages will contain what I've learned so far, but I readily admit that I'm still a work in progress. "Nancy + Aaron" is my current course of study. I've continued to learn and grow during the process of writing this book, and I'll be sharing my insights and experiences with you transparently in real time.

ARE YOU READY FOR A BETTER RELATIONSHIP MODEL?

Now . . . what about you? Are you ready to turn the spotlight on relationship and move to the *next level*—a kind of relationship more fulfilling than you've had before?

Whether you know it or not, if you're reading this book, you're on an awakening path. Maybe you've *jumped* and created a new life for yourself. Maybe you've found your way to *worthy*, increasing both your self-worth and your net worth. Perhaps the next frontier is relationship—the most potent spiritual "school" we have in our day and age.

Wherever you are in your personal development journey, this book is for you if you find yourself in any of the following situations:

If you're single and . . .

- Looking for a new relationship that's a level beyond what you've experienced before.

- Happy to be alone for now, but want to prepare for a future great relationship—a healthier one than you've had in the past.

- Divorced or reeling from a breakup, feeling determined never to do that again.

- Recovering from the death of a partner, feeling unsure what to do next.

Or you're currently in a relationship . . .

- That clearly needs an upgrade.

- That requires you to cross your own boundaries in order to stay.

- That you recognize to be the exact right teacher for you, even if it's confronting. (This is where I find myself with Aaron.)

- That's no longer satisfying your heart's longing, but you want to find a way to stay and be happy.

- That feels stagnant, and you aren't sure if you should stay or go.

Essentially, this book is for you if you want something more in relationship than what the old models have offered.

This Book Is *Not* for You If . . .

You're in a relationship where there is physical or emotional violence. If this is what you're experiencing, please put this book on the shelf for now and pick up my book *Jump . . . And Your Life Will Appear*, or seek the help of a therapist.

NOT YOUR AVERAGE RELATIONSHIP BOOK

Just like my book *Worthy* was different from most finance books on the market, this book differs significantly from the majority of relationship books out there. First and foremost, this isn't a "dating" book. I won't show you how to attract a partner or how to impress. I won't offer you tips and tricks for navigating the online dating world. I won't help you write a great personal ad or determine which ads you should respond to. I won't provide a how-to guide for finding your dream partner or manifesting your soul mate. More important, this book isn't about learning to shut down your emotional triggers so that you can have a seemingly more harmonious relationship. While you may find yourself in a deeply satisfying relationship on the other side of reading this book, it's not going to be because you've learned how to make yourself into someone you're not.

What this book *will* offer you is:

- A process for maintaining a sense of self while you're in partnership with someone else.

- A way to show up in your relationships without projecting your past onto the present.

- A path toward healthy relationships, driven by authenticity and intimacy rather than fear.

- A guidebook for the new relationship blueprint—one that turns the old relationship model of "you complete me" on its head.

By the time you've worked through this book, you'll know what you're looking for in Relationship 2.0, and/or how to upgrade the relationship you already have.

This Book Applies to All Relationships

The job of writing an inclusive book about relationships using the limited tool of the English language is a daunting one. Our language is itself biased and black-or-white, leaving little room for the beautiful diversity and ambiguity that make up our actual world.

Since the overwhelming majority of my clients happen to be heterosexual females, those are the stories that primarily populate this book. But the principles here apply to all relationships regardless of gender. They even apply to relationships beyond romance, including business partnerships, friendships, and familial bonds.

I simply made the choice to allow the audience that has already found my work to speak for themselves on these pages because these are the authentic stories that have organically come out of this work . . . *so far.* In spite of that, it's my sincere hope that their voices will touch your heart and life, even if the relationships described look a bit different from your own.

IT ACTUALLY COMES DOWN TO ONE THING

Before we continue, I need to make an important point. There's a Trojan horse in all the work I do: Regardless of the subject matter, *it's all about self-love.*

In my humble opinion, this whole *life* is a lesson in self-love.

But it's really easy to forget that, especially when it comes to relationship issues. Instead, we blame others or beat ourselves up when we perceive our relationships as not working. Note that I said *"perceive* our relationships as not working." Sometimes, our attachment to Hollywood romance—the "you complete me" syndrome—causes us to have unrealistic expectations of our relationships. We define a good relationship as one in which there's no conflict, no difficulty. When our emotional "stuff" arises, it's easier to believe we "just haven't found the right mate" than to face the prospect that our own deeper personal growth work may be calling us.

The secret to a powerful, loving relationship isn't about fixing or enduring problems. It isn't about improving ourselves in order to "overcome." Nope. It all boils down to this*: Once we truly love ourselves, and make ourselves a priority, everything becomes possible.*

In fact, you can stop reading the book if you truly get this point: *Relationship is first and foremost where we learn how to love ourselves.* Contrary to popular belief, learning how to love others is *not* the top priority. I couldn't possibly have the relationship I have now if I hadn't awakened to myself first. Again, relationship is where we learn how to love *ourselves.*

You're going to forget that, but it's okay. We all do. I'm going to remind you as you continue reading, but mark my words: *I've just given you everything you need to know to have the relationship you truly desire.*

HOW TO USE THIS BOOK

In the chapters that follow, I'll give you a 10-step process for working through your underlying emotional and psychological roadblocks to self-love and the relationship you want. I'll share more of my own story, and you'll read about many of my clients who have made big shifts in their lives and their relationships. Along the way, you'll do the same exercises I give my clients to discover what's standing in the way of a better relationship—first with yourself and then with others.

Here's the plan:

Step 1: Reframe Relationship as Spiritual Path. This first step is about learning how to take a mature approach to relationship, knowing that no relationship is going to save you. Instead, it's meant to *grow* you.

Step 2: Identify Your Relationship Beliefs. In this step, you'll look at your "origin story" from childhood and determine the beliefs about relationships that you developed as a result. Then you'll replace your old beliefs with new, more empowering ones.

Step 3: Revisit Your Relationship History. This step is about mining your past history to find the repeating patterns that have played out in your relationships over time. We'll also explore the underlying commitments that may be standing in the way of the relationship you want.

Step 4: Make Peace with Your Past . . . and Let It Go. This step is about making peace with your past through forgiveness of others, self-forgiveness, and gratitude. Specific exercises will help you let go of what has come before and set the stage for moving forward.

Step 5: Redefine Intimacy. To most people, "intimacy" means "sex," but the truth is that you can have sex without any intimacy whatsoever. True intimacy is synonymous with closeness, sharing, collaborative insight, revelation, and authenticity. It requires vulnerability and honesty. In this step, we'll explore intimacy as the foundation of relationship, starting with your relationship to yourself.

Step 6: Embrace Selfishness. This chapter's step may challenge your idea of what "selfish" and "selfless" mean.

We'll talk about how taking care of your own needs first actually makes you a better partner and improves the quality of your relationship.

Step 7: Go It Alone for a While. In this step, I'll suggest that you take a sabbatical from relationship with others in order to deepen your relationship with self. If you're in a relationship or you're a parent, you'll simply take a short self-guided retreat. If you're single, I'll suggest you take a month off from dating. It's a critical "pattern interrupt" on the journey toward the new relationship blueprint.

Step 8: Hone Your New Relationship Skills. This step is about learning to navigate the challenges that inevitably arise when you share your life with another human being. You'll take what you've learned about the new relationship blueprint and begin to see how it can be applied in your world.

Step 9: Envision the Relationship You Desire. Here, you'll envision the relationship you truly desire. What would you like to *feel* in relationship with someone else? How does the relationship look? You'll explore whether, like some of my clients, you've tried to force yourself into a conventional relationship that hasn't actually worked for you or your partner—and whether a more unconventional relationship would make you happier and more fulfilled.

Step 10: Lean into Love. This last step is about leaning into loving yourself first, before expressing your love to someone else. This is the ultimate lesson, whether you're already in a relationship, looking for one, or happily single. I told you I'd get back to this! When self-love is missing, you can't feel the love coming from others. It's like your laptop doesn't have a port for the "love" cord.

You might think you're going to feel love from the outside in, but you have to feel it on the inside first.

If these steps sound daunting, don't worry! I'm going to be right here with you the whole way. There will be meditations and writing exercises in each chapter to help you integrate what you've learned. Each step will prepare you for the one that follows, and you can go as slowly as you need. The rewards will be well worth your effort. And I know you can do it!

Do You Need to Write Down the Exercises?

Yes! There will be quite a few exercises in each chapter, and it's important that you write down your answers. I'll ask you to refer to them at times, so you'll need to be able to find what you wrote.

You can record your answers on your computer or other device, or you can write them in a paper journal.

I encourage you to also write down any additional thoughts and feelings that come up for you as you read the book and complete the exercises. This is a journey of self-discovery, and if you take the time to reflect on what you write, you'll learn a lot about yourself. Often when we go back and reread journals from a few days, weeks, or months ago, we gain important insights that can help us see and let go of limiting beliefs. Writing is a powerful process, so use it to your advantage as you engage with these pages.

MY INVITATION TO YOU

I invite you to trust that you can "do love" differently. You can do it again without doing it the same as before.

You *can* have a relationship that's loving and healing after the one that fell apart or broke your heart.

This is a choice point. You can choose love without losing yourself. You can be nourished in the holding and being held and in the giving and receiving. Truth-telling, making yourself a priority, and cozying up to conflict will guide you to find your "no" so that you can free your "yes." Trust that intimate relationship can be a "container" that holds the truth of who each of you is and be strong enough to hold your differences, too.

I invite you to join my Facebook group, Transform Together: Nancy Levin Insiders, at www.nancylevininsiders .com to discuss your experiences as you move through the book. You'll get a lot of support from others who are on similar journeys, and you'll feel less alone as your process unfolds.

Take my hand, and let's get started.

Step 1

Reframe Relationship as Spiritual Path

"I've been thinking that I'd like to go to Thailand for five weeks in November for a meditation retreat," Aaron said to me one day in the summer of 2015. "What do you think? Will you come with me?"

"Five weeks? *Five weeks?*" I said. "There's no way I could take that much time off. That's too much!"

Even now, thinking about going away for five whole weeks is almost enough to make me hyperventilate. Not since I was 25 years old had I taken a non-business-related trip for anywhere near that length of time.

But for Aaron, such a trip is no big deal. He has lived in Aspen, Colorado, for 25 years, where it's normal to work the two high seasons and take off the other two seasons. Ski town people are always making plans for off-season getaways to exotic locales, and Aaron was inviting me into his world. But that's never been my lifestyle. I prefer responsibility. Plus, as I mentioned, I'm a workaholic. Even when I worked as the Event Director for Hay House, I didn't take my paid days off. I accrued so many vacation days over my years there that I could have taken *months* off!

So it's no surprise that during this conversation, Aaron's face seemed to morph into my ex-husband's face. It was as if the Aaron I knew and loved had disappeared. I couldn't hear his voice anymore; all I could hear was my ex's voice.

The fear tied itself into a knot inside me. Would I have to do what Aaron wanted? Would Aaron end up needing me to take care of him like my ex did? Would I lose myself in this relationship and fall into my old patterns?

I knew this was Aaron, not my ex. But the same triggers around laziness, not feeling supported, and believing I had to abandon myself for love were all right there. Why? Because, as I said in the Introduction, both of these relationships had a common denominator: *me.* These were *my* triggers, and it didn't matter who I was in relationship with. These triggers would show up because they're mine to work through. Mine to heal.

Thankfully, because of what I learned during the course of my marriage and what I'm learning as a result of being in relationship with Aaron, I was able to notice that my irrational fear was coming onto the scene. I was able to let Aaron know that this part of me was present, rather than lashing out at him reactively. I was able to reply with compassion to the frightened part of me.

"I'll never let myself take care of another partner financially," I assured myself. "And I'm not abandoning anyone, especially not myself. If I agree to take this trip, it will be because I want the experience, and I'd like to nurture my relationship at the same time. I'll only take it if I determine it will enhance my life, love, and work."

After some contemplation, I told Aaron, "I'll go for three weeks, but only if we do a meditation retreat. I don't want to just travel around for weeks without a productive purpose. If we can do a retreat, I'd love to be there with you."

He loved the idea. In the end, I got on the plane, and we spent three wonderful weeks in Thailand.

As I write this, we're back in Moab, Utah, for three weeks. Aaron isn't working, because it's his off season, but I am. It's interesting to watch him go about his day with no set schedule and nothing he *has* to do. My judgments arise and my irrational fear of having to support him along with it. He would like me to be more available for fun activities, which again runs counter to my natural tendency to work all the time. But I wouldn't be with someone like Aaron if I didn't need and want to cultivate the ability to be playful, spend more time at leisure, and let go of an irrational fear of being irresponsible. So Aaron is the perfect mirror for another part of me that wants expression. I'm terrified to let go and play, but Aaron is the perfect teacher—helping me to become more balanced. Our relationship has helped me understand that fun and success aren't mutually exclusive and that leisure doesn't automatically mean laziness.

Using our relationships to see, notice, and then work with our emotional reactivity is just one way the new relationship blueprint operates as spiritual path. It's a powerful way of discovering our unresolved issues so that we can move closer to balance within ourselves. The relationship itself becomes a crucible—a container for growth—that gives us the opportunity to do our personal development work in an everyday sort of way.

This first step in renovating your relationship blueprint is to take a mature view of the purpose of relating. Relationship isn't meant to save you; it's meant to *grow you*.

What Is a Spiritual Path?

The term *spiritual path* has a different meaning for each of us, so let me explain what it means for me in relation to this book. I'm not talking about chasing enlightenment or developing a relationship with the divine. Those are great endeavors, but that's not what I'm after here.

For me, a spiritual path is about *transformation*, not *transcendence*. You might call it more of a *psycho*spiritual path, in that it's about doing our psychological work as much as our spiritual work.

For me, spirituality is about becoming more peaceful, present, at ease, and truthful with ourselves and others. Seeing and embracing the truth is key, because only then can we accept who we are with all of our foibles and humanity. Buddha once said, "You know the Truth, because the Truth works." When we accept the truth, our lives and our relationships work better.

A spiritual path as I define it also trains us to respond to situations in our lives with love instead of fear. That starts with turning our love toward ourselves, before we turn it toward others.

To reach these goals, we have to become aware of our negative triggers and fears so that we can work to clear them. You'll learn more about how to do that as you continue with the steps of the book.

If your version of a spiritual path is something other than what I've just described, you can give our work together another name like "relational awakening" or "the path of increased awareness." What you call it doesn't matter as long as we're on the same page about what it means within the context of the book.

DROP THE MYTH THAT RELATIONSHIP WILL SAVE YOU

In the not-so-distant past, people got married for very practical reasons. Marriage was a stabilizing societal force. It was a way to have children legitimately, and for many generations, it was a necessity for the survival of women, who weren't allowed to own property or work. Some reasons people have used for being in relationship based on the "old" model include:

- To have sex/live together
- To have kids
- To be taken care of
- To divide or share the labor
- To meet societal or family expectations

Then, in the 18th century in Western cultures, romantic love became more often the reason we entered intimate, committed relationships. Since then, we've been fueled by fairy tales of being rescued from drudgery like Cinderella or awakened from a long sleep by the magic of a kiss like Sleeping Beauty. We women have envisioned ourselves as damsels to be rescued, while men pictured themselves as heroes riding up on white horses.

Classic literature, modern music, and movies have done us no favors either. We've mooned over the obsessive love of Cathy and Heathcliff in *Wuthering Heights* with its "I can't survive without you" mentality. Love songs have taught us that passion is all about somehow blending into each other until there are no boundaries left. This has left us conditioned to believe that we aren't in love unless we lose ourselves. While a certain amount of surrender to love is both necessary and beneficial, giving ourselves up to another person is not.

Then there's the "finding The One" mentality, under-written by countless movies and romance novels. But have you noticed how almost all romantic comedies end right before all the hard stuff begins? By the "hard stuff," I mean the reality of living together day to day, among the stresses of paying the bills and taking care of the kids. Not to mention all the psycho-emotional baggage we all carry with us from childhood.

So many of the people I've coached, both men and women, have assimilated the belief that if they find "The One," they won't ever have to feel lonely, sad, or rejected again. We look for a relationship that will provide us with validation and approval. But that's a myth, and that myth is a trap. My apologies if I'm breaking bad news here, but relationship won't prevent you from feeling any of those unpleasant emotions. The only person who can ease your feelings of loneliness, sadness, or rejection is *you*. The only person who can validate you and give you the approval you seek is *you*.

I do believe that "true love" and easy relationship are possible for people who have already done the hard work of learning these lessons. But the truth is that until you love and accept yourself, no one else's validation is going to stick. You'll *want* to believe their praise, but you won't believe it at the deepest unconscious levels. Because of this, you'll just need validation again the next day . . . and the next day . . . and the next. Have you ever known anyone who needed to be validated all the time? It's exhausting.

That's what I meant when I said that healthy rela-tionship is really about loving yourself. Relationships remain on shaky ground when you require someone else to determine your worthiness. That's because no one else can guarantee your worth. You're inherently worthy, and it's up to you to take that in and truly believe it.

Exercise #1: What's Your Relationship Myth?

Let's dive into our first exercise and begin to get an idea of what you've told yourself about relationships that may or may not be true. We'll call this your own personal "relationship myth." You'll learn more about your myth as you continue reading and working with the exercises.

For this exercise, complete each of the following sentences at least five times, with five different endings. Try to answer these questions as the version of yourself you were prior to doing any personal development work. Believe it or not, the stories we developed in childhood and our teenage years are the hardest to let go because they've been with us the longest. If you can think of more answers, please continue beyond that. Write down whatever pops into your head, without censoring or explaining.

Here's an example:

A story I've told myself about relationships is . . . *that they can completely fulfill me.*

The reality has been . . . *that relationships haven't fulfilled me at all. Even when I gave my all to a relationship, I still didn't feel fulfilled.*

1. A story I've told myself about relationships is

    _____.

    The reality has been _____

    _____.

2. A story I've told myself about relationships is
    _____.
    The reality has been _____
    _____.

3. A story I've told myself about relationships is
    _____.
    The reality has been _____
    _____.

4. A story I've told myself about relationships is
    _____.
    The reality has been _____
    _____.

5. A story I've told myself about relationships is
    _____.
    The reality has been _____
    _____.

These stories make up your "relationship myth." Be sure to hold on to your answers so that you can refer to them later.

RELATIONSHIP IS SCHOOL

As I said, this new blueprint reframes relationship as spiritual path. Another way of saying that is: Relationship is school. In fact, *relationship is the number-one school for personal growth and spiritual development in our modern world.* Our relationships are teachers that help us become more whole, conscious human beings.

Sure, you can try to avoid ever getting your triggers hit by avoiding relationships altogether—like I did after my divorce. But unless you become a hermit, your soul is going to make sure those triggers get activated by *someone*. That's the case with my friend Alice. She hasn't been in a romantic relationship for a few years. Then, suddenly, some of the issues she used to have with men started to show up in her relationship with her best girlfriend. The soul wants to evolve, and it's going to get its learning one way or another. I believe trying to avoid relationship is counter to what we're meant to do here as spiritual beings having a human experience.

The truth is that intimate relationships give us the absolute best schoolroom for our growth. They bring out the best in us because we love so deeply, but they also bring out the worst in us because they cause us to bump up against our defenses and fears. As I've said, we draw to us partners who trigger us the most. They show us the disowned parts of ourselves, like Aaron has shown me how I tend to disown my ability to be "lazy" and have fun.

So if you've ever wondered why the same issues tend to come up in relationship after relationship—or repeatedly in your current relationship—it's because those issues are the core of your curriculum. You'll *always* unconsciously orchestrate the exact relationship you need in order to learn what your soul wants you to learn in this life. If you need to learn that you're lovable, you'll feel rejected over and over. If you need to learn that your body is beautiful, you'll draw partners who criticize those few extra pounds. If you need to learn how to own your own space in the world, you'll repeatedly choose relationships where you have to fight for your voice to be heard. Your soul sees relationship as a perfect opportunity to finally break free of wounds and fears that have kept you in chains, probably for years. So if you find yourself attracting or attracted to relationships in which you see the same issues over and over, it's because you still have work to do to break free of those issues.

When we don't approach relationship as a spiritual path and listen to the messages our soul sends us from our partner, our triggers derail us emotionally. We keep making the same choices, actions, and decisions, so the future shows up just like the past. Then our relationships often fall apart in a painful way, and we end up facing those same patterns in our next partnership.

When we approach relationship as a spiritual path, however, we seek the truth Buddha was talking about. This allows relationship to help us reclaim and heal our shadow selves—the parts of us that we haven't yet been willing to see or the parts that have been hurt and afraid. As we integrate our disowned parts, our triggers become less intense. As a result, life is more peaceful and more enjoyable, even as we deal with the challenges that our soul continues to present to us in our "relationship schoolroom."

I've found that viewing my relationship as a spiritual path has allowed me to have a provocative and stimulating partnership with Aaron that enhances my life in so many ways. In my marriage, I couldn't see the lessons that I needed to learn. I spent all of my time trying to prevent the triggers, rather than allowing them to arise and working with them consciously. As a result, I lost contact with my needs and desires, and ultimately with myself.

But I also know that reframing relationship as spiritual path doesn't mean that some partnerships won't fall apart. It doesn't mean we won't have painful experiences in relationship. We might need to move on to a new schoolroom with a new partner. Or we might need some time on our own to regroup.

This new relationship blueprint gives us a way of looking at relationships that can help us observe the pain and pull ourselves out of it more quickly. When you and your partner can see the issues between you as part of your growth, you're less likely to cast blame or lose yourself to irrationality. And the good news is that as soon as you bring an issue into your awareness, you've already begun the healing process just by virtue of that awareness.

Now hold on a minute, you may be thinking. Am I saying that the *only* purpose of relationship is school? What about human connection, companionship, family, and reaching mutual goals together? Don't worry, I see the value in all of these wonderful things, too. As I said, my relationship with Aaron has enhanced my life in many ways. And we *do* have fun, despite the part of me that sometimes fights it. Relationships are also about companionship, love, sex, intimacy, shared experience, support, and even validation. Yes, you can get validation and support from your relationship, and I hope you do! The problem arises when you *rely* on your relationship for validation or support, or if you expect it to be your *only* source of validation and support. I hope I don't sound harsh when I say this, but in the end, we can't rely on another human being—not even a partner or spouse—to take care of our emotional needs. Relying on an external source for our internal well-being sets us up for disappointment and pain. The late author H. W. L. Poonja once said, "Expectations are never fulfilled. If you expect, then you are in bondage."

As I mentioned in the Introduction, Aaron and I have set a relationship "container" that allows us to hold on to our love, even when we trigger each other—becoming angry, resentful, sad, or hurt. Because we're aware that we're working through our innermost issues, we don't look at these negative emotions as signs that our relationship is problematic and needs to end. Instead, we've consciously designated our relationship as a place where it's safe to experience these emotions that weren't safe to experience in childhood. We want our relationship to have the capacity, elasticity, and resiliency to hold both of us in our truth, in our differences, and in our discomfort—all of it.

If we feel the emotions and look at them with curiosity in order to learn more about ourselves, we can allow the feelings to move through us rather than get stuck. On the other hand, if we hold on to our feelings of anger, hurt, betrayal, or abandonment rather than examining and releasing them, we put the relationship at risk.

By serving as a mirror for what our soul wants us to see, our significant others are our greatest teachers and most wonderful gifts. In relationship, we not only receive companionship and intimacy, but we also have an opportunity to heal our core wounds and expand the consciousness of our soul. Relationship as spiritual path means that we can access a level of healing that we simply can't access on our own.

Relationship Reframe

"I let go of the myth that relationship will save me and reframe relationship as spiritual path."

Step 2

Identify Your Relationship Beliefs

I was born into a mourning family, a grieving family. When I was two years old, my six-year-old brother died of pneumonia. He had been born mentally incapacitated, so he had problems right from the beginning.

Then, four years after my brother came along—and with nine months of swimming around in my mother's neuroses and fear—I entered a world in which both of my parents were focused on helping my brother survive. Understandably, he had to be their number-one priority.

What happens to the second child in a situation like that? Well, before I could even verbalize it, I understood that my brother's wants and needs were far more important than mine. I knew I'd better not have any wants and needs of my own. I believed I'd better become self-sufficient and independent . . . *fast!*

My parents loved me, while also watching me from a bit of a distance to make sure nothing would turn out to be wrong with me. After all, my brother's condition didn't become evident until he failed to develop the way other babies do. When he didn't roll over, lift his head, or sit up at the appropriate times, they knew something was wrong.

They must have been so relieved when I developed at a normal pace. But as a tiny girl, all I could think was that something *must* be wrong with me if I was under such scrutiny.

My mother has told me in recent years that she was afraid to become attached to me for the first few months in case I suffered from the same condition as my brother. I certainly understand why, but I can't say it didn't have an impact. Without the usual mother-child bonding that happens immediately after birth, I was even more certain that something was wrong with me. Even more sure that I had to be self-sufficient, in spite of how well my parents cared for me.

When my brother died, I concluded that being imperfect—being broken in any way—equals death. If I didn't want to die, I had to make absolutely certain that *nothing* was wrong with me. Thus began my quest for perfection and what I call my "Superwoman complex."

This is my "origin story," which imprinted on my psyche and set the course of my life . . . and my future relationships. It also caused me to unconsciously create survival strategies. Perfectionism was one of them.

My brother died when I was only two. The little girl in me "made it mean" that perfectionism was the only way she could stay alive. In my young mind's "meaning-making machine," it truly was life or death. Outwardly it wasn't true, but it became my inner truth—my "programming."

We misinterpret our childhood experiences because we have so little life experience with which to compare them. Plus, our brains are so malleable that we have little ability to evaluate circumstances logically. These meanings—these misinterpretations—become powerful beliefs that we carry with us throughout our lives. They're the root of our relationship myths and the stories we tell ourselves. Even though an objective observer could see in a second how groundless our stories are, the stories persist in our own hearts and minds. We literally build our lives on top of them, and they're as invisible to us as water is to a fish while it's swimming in it. I call these foundational ideas "shadow beliefs," "limiting beliefs," or "false beliefs."

So there I was, growing up, trying with all my might to be perfect. Perfection equaled outward praise, so I tracked for things others would see and notice—grades, perfect attendance, and a clean bedroom. (I was a kid, after all.) Joy and fun never won anybody a gold star, so they got coded as frivolous and irresponsible. That was my map of life from childhood onward, and it's the map I was using the day I met the man who would become my husband.

As discussed in Step 1, I attracted the person whose core wounds were a perfect match for my own. Our core wounds are the deepest, most profound sources of pain inside of us. They stem from our origin story, and we usually attract someone who "activates" those wounds. One of my core wounds is that if I'm *not* perfect, I'll die. Another core wound, formed around the same story, is that no one will ever take care of me.

As I said, I became tenaciously independent. Not because I wanted to, but because I felt I had no choice. My ex, of course, was just the opposite. He had a profound need to be taken care of, a pattern forged in childhood when he didn't get the loving care he and every child needs and deserves.

I could've learned the lessons from my marriage much sooner if I'd only had the awareness at that time (or this book!). Instead, I tried hard to be perfect in my marriage. Louise Hay once told me that I deserved an Academy Award for my portrayal of the "perfect wife." Still, no matter how hard I tried, I wasn't perfect enough in my husband's eyes. The more he demanded, the more I demanded of myself—making my own wants and needs irrelevant, just as I had when I was a child. My brand of perfection had always meant trying to "fix" everybody around me. If I was perfect, maybe I could heal his pain. Then we'd both feel safe.

In striving for that false image of perfection, though, I sacrificed my true self. If I'd had the self-worth and awareness I needed at that time, I'd have realized that I was trying to climb an unclimbable mountain. Moreover, I would have seen very quickly that I was in an unhealthy relationship that needed to be over.

So if I'd been the woman I am today, I would have ended the marriage much sooner. But I didn't yet have that awareness or self-love. And this is the most important part: As long as I was still running the story that I needed to be perfect, would never be taken care of, and had to subjugate my own needs and desires to be loved, I couldn't help but draw toward me a relationship that would prove me correct.

There was a moment when the pain became too much to bear, but I still couldn't see a healthy way out. So what did I do? While I was still married, I found a man who accepted me as I was, with all of my imperfections. It was a feeling I hadn't experienced before, and it was intoxicating to the extreme. Against my better judgment—and to my great shame—I entered into an affair. I'm not at all proud of that choice, but I've since forgiven myself.

I've now learned that when you don't express your truth directly, it always comes out sideways.

Nevertheless, it wasn't until years after the affair was over that my husband found out about it. He read my journals while I was out of town, and all hell broke loose. In my case, "hell" was pain, blame, and shame like I'd never known was possible. Once again, my story was proven true: If I'm not perfect, I will suffer mercilessly. I was loyal to that belief, and so stayed in the toxic environment of my deteriorating marriage for two more years.

This is exactly the kind of hell that will break loose when we don't do the work of exploring our core wounds consciously and with awareness. Until we're ready to look at, and feel through, all the pain we experienced as children, we'll stay blind to our own behavioral patterns that are creating our own version of hell. We're at the mercy of our false beliefs, and it's difficult to bring the life we most want to fruition.

Since I didn't have the exploration I'm going to walk you through in this book, it took all hell breaking loose in my marriage to begin to bring my beliefs into awareness. Only once I saw how my own beliefs were the cause of my pain could I move into a healthier way of being. Unfortunately, that meant a contentious divorce. My hope is that the process in this book will help you avoid a similar fate.

Of course, wherever you are in your relationship story—happily partnered, unhappily partnered, single, divorced, or widowed—I can't promise you that because you have this book in your hands you won't experience drama. Life is infinitely dramatic. But if you take my hand and give yourself the gift of discovering your innermost secrets, you might be able to avoid a big blowup. At the very least, I know that awareness, acceptance of the truth, self-forgiveness, and self-love help soften the blow.

That's why Step 2 is about *identifying your relationship beliefs*—because until you excavate the unconscious material that's running the show in the background, you can't change your relationship story.

You've already begun to unearth some of these beliefs by writing down the stories you tell yourself. But in this step, we'll go much deeper.

Get Support If You Need It!

During the course of this chapter and beyond, you'll delve into your past and do a lot of writing. Please take care of yourself! If you find that you need some emotional support while you complete the exercises, see a therapist, ask a friend to lend an ear, or find online support.

Just remember that feelings are passing visitors, and you cleanse pieces of your core wounds each time you cry or express anger in a healthy way. Then you make room for more peace and joy to come in. So express whatever comes up in the moment by letting the tears flow, or screaming into a pillow (or punching it or throwing it across the room . . . just try not to hit anything valuable!). To whatever degree you can, try to let the feelings run their course. Holding on to them could result in "sideways" behaviors—like my affair—which can harm your loved ones, your co-workers, or yourself.

Most important is to love yourself to the best of your ability as you work through this process. It will be an enlightening and empowering experience. When you're finished with this step alone, I suspect you'll know yourself better than you ever have.

Exercise #2: Your Origin Story

In this exercise, you'll begin to unearth your own origin story. The exercise has two parts and begins with a short meditation, so you'll need time and space to be quiet, in addition to paper, a journal, or computer/tablet to record your answers to the written portion.

Part 1—Childhood Memory Meditation

I know it can be difficult to remember your childhood and even harder to figure out what your programming told you. So let's first do a 15- to 20-minute meditation to help jog your memory and put you back in that time period. If your childhood was particularly traumatic, take a moment to speak to your inner child and remind him/her that what happened is in the past. It really is just a memory, and you're safe right now in this moment. Remind the child within that you, as the adult, are here for protection.

Since this part is a meditation, be sure to turn off all phones so that you can surrender to the process. Wear comfortable clothes, and sit on a comfortable chair or couch. Feel free to play soft music or light candles, if you like. It helps to record your own voice reading the steps so that you don't have to open your eyes, which will disrupt your meditative state. Note that if you record your own version, you may want to leave out the italicized portions of the script.

Note, too, that the opening part of the meditation will be the same for all meditations within the book. This is so you can become accustomed to the relaxation portion and make moving into a meditative state second nature.

1. Close your eyes, and take several breaths. Relax each part of your body, starting with your feet. Then, gradually move up your legs, hips, belly, chest, back, arms, neck, and head

until you feel fully relaxed. *Don't work too hard at this. Just ask your body to relax. As you continue, it will relax more and more.*

2. When you're ready, with your eyes closed picture or feel yourself in the home you lived in when you were four years old. Allow yourself to smell the scents, hear the sounds, and feel the air. Once you feel anchored in the experience of your childhood, ask yourself the question: "What's my earliest memory?" Then, wait for something to come into your mind. It might be a word, a picture, or a full scene. Don't worry if you don't visualize anything. You might simply have a sense or feeling of some kind. Allow for whatever comes forward. If you draw a blank, take a deep breath and try asking the question again. Sometimes we try too hard, and that gets in the way. If that happens, it can help to ask a few times with a deep breath in between. Just wait a few seconds each time to allow impressions to form in whatever way they want.

3. Now take another deep breath and drop down into an even deeper relaxed state. Ask yourself: "What's my first memory about relationships?" Allow any pictures or feelings to come to you. Maybe you'll envision your parents or other adults interacting with each other. Maybe you'll see or sense yourself as a child with a friend or a sibling.

4. Spend as much time as you like with your memories. Then open your eyes and come back to the present moment. Take time to write down what you saw or felt so that you

don't forget. Please take notes even if you're sure you'll remember. You'll be glad you did!

5. *If the memories cause any unpleasant feelings, first and foremost be kind to yourself. With any self-inquiry, you're waking up parts of yourself that have been dormant. In many cases they've been consciously or unconsciously pushed aside for the sake of self-preservation. In the work we're doing, you're going to stop pushing those parts aside and consciously move into the fullness of who you are. So be present with your emotions. Cry if you need to cry, punch that pillow, talk to a friend, and/or write in your journal. Acknowledging your feelings can begin to transform their energy and ease their intensity. My client Claire told me that she had never said "I'm sad" out loud until recently. Once she acknowledged her sadness, the emotions started to flow—and she felt great relief. When the emotions begin to subside, be as gentle with yourself for the remainder of the day and evening as you can.*

Part 2—Writing Your Origin Story

Now that we've jogged your memory with the meditation, it's time to write down the events of your own origin story—your version of the one I shared at the beginning of the chapter. To the best of your ability, write down the key moments or experiences you remember about your childhood, the ones that may have been formative. You don't have to know yet what beliefs you formed as a result of what happened. We'll do that next. For now, just write down the events you remember, and keep the list handy so that you can refer to it later.

HOW YOUR BELIEFS BECOME THE DIRECTOR OF YOUR RELATIONSHIP STORY

Your origin story has been directing your relationship history, much like the director of a movie. The beliefs you created during those formative years draw toward you the people, relationships, and situations that reinforce those beliefs. For example, if you unconsciously believe that men can't be trusted, you'll likely attract men who can't be trusted, or you'll destroy relationships with your own lack of trust. Even if you don't verbalize it, the energy will be there, and your partner will feel the distrust unconsciously.

How does this happen, exactly? I'll be honest and say that it remains a mystery to me. I can't explain, for example, how a woman chooses a man who is sober when she meets him, only for him to become an alcoholic just like her father once they're married. I will leave it up to each of us to explain the "how" in our own way.

But to set change in motion, all we really need to know is the "why." See if you can identify with the "why" in the following origin stories, which come from my clients.

* * *

Emily learned early on that no one was going to be able to hear her voice over "the endless screaming, name-calling, blaming, and things flying around" in her childhood home. "I learned that people can't have differences and cohabitate," she says. "They either agree with each other and are therefore in love, or they disagree with each other and therefore hate each other. As a result of receiving these false messages in childhood, my own relationships had no room for autonomy, authenticity, or differences of any kind. Any differences between us triggered

22

deep-seated insecurities within me, and I took them personally as judgments against me. As a result, there has been a 'fight or flight' theme to all of my relationships."

Like Emily, Lily's childhood household was in constant conflict, and there were plenty of contradictions to confuse her young mind. "There was weird stuff like Mom putting me down if I dared excel more than my older brother at school or sport, as boys were supposedly superior. It was hard holding myself back. Mom held the seat of power at home, despite the fact that according to her law that men were superior, Dad should have held the power."

Some of the beliefs that Lily formed in childhood were that people are cruel and tell lies, "even the people who are supposed to care for you," she says. "Relationships are battlefields. It was safer and more peaceful to keep to myself than get caught up in Mom's dramas, as I was always in trouble for talking to the wrong person or saying the wrong thing. So if you tell people what you really want, they'll only use it against you. Wow, no wonder I have trouble asking for what I want or need!"

Brenda has a similar pattern to mine. After she was born, her family adopted her younger sister, who was quite handicapped. "So in my house," she says, "the kids who were independent were strong and ignored, and the kids who needed help got all the attention. I realized that if I could be a people-pleaser, I could get more attention. That led to a recurring issue of not celebrating any successes in my life for fear that people would think I didn't need anything. Even today, I feel like if I celebrate my success, I'll let my guard down and lose the attention I crave."

Grace's parents played very traditional roles. "Mom didn't work outside the home. She was the primary day-to-day parent," Grace says. "I didn't notice much physical affection between my parents. No passion and excitement for each other. When they were together, they related to each other in a somewhat disconnected but calm way. As the years went on, the disconnect deepened, communication broke down, the marriage failed, and they divorced when I was 23. My mom felt my dad was emotionally dead, mean, and disrespectful. Dad had no clue, I don't think. In my opinion, when Mom was finally able to express her needs and dissatisfaction, it was too late, and Dad didn't know how to handle it. Then he declared war, shut down bank accounts, took inventory of household items, and went into almost a military defensive mode. He played hardball, retaliating with stipulations that my mom support herself after a certain amount of time. I felt this was an undue hardship since she had no marketable skills due to their traditional roles. She had been dedicated to him for over 30 years. My mom was lost, deeply hurt, fragile, and unstable as a result. She struggled emotionally and financially and never fully recovered."

What did Grace make all of this mean? "Love is unpredictable and unreliable. With love comes pain and disappointment. The happiness won't last. Someone always has to be subordinate; the needs of both can't be met simultaneously. Also, sacrifice is part of love, and the degree of sacrifice is evidence of the strength of love."

For Leah, relationships always seemed to be about dominance and compliance. "There were always complaints about something not done right, in a certain way, or at the right time," she says. "Always a criticism about everything and everybody. That left me believing I had to be compliant and perfect in order to be loved. There were a lot of outbursts, leaving me in fear of speaking up and being seen. It was always best just to keep the peace.

I thought if I did things for others with perfection and kept to myself, then and only then would they love me."

Stella watched her dad give her mom the silent treatment if she badgered him too much, so Stella became the peacekeeper between her parents. She says she developed these beliefs about relationships: "It's a bartering process. If you do this for me, I'll do that for you. Forget about being our authentic selves. We need to change who we are to accommodate the other person. You won't be able to stand it when someone is mad at you. You have to have peace at all times."

"I'm a military brat," my client Charles says. "Dad was gone 90 percent of the time. It was just my mother, my sister, and me. My mother eventually got to the point where she was tired of being the at-home mom. So she stepped out and started her business career. That was when I stepped into the role of taking care of the family while Dad was away. It was always 'What can I do for you?' or 'What would you like?' It was never 'I would like this' or 'This is what I want.'" As a result, Charles came to believe that he had to justify his existence by taking care of others, especially his significant other.

Jocelyn says, "As a child, I would visit my dad in the summer. My mom would drill into my head not to get in the car if he was drinking. The choice of doing so literally had life or death consequences. Now, as an adult, I make every choice seem like life or death. So I make safe choices. I don't fully commit. I don't show up as passionately and alive as I am. I dim my light to be safe."

Maria's origin story led her to believe that "one person—the 'weaker' one—has to cater to the 'stronger' one." In other words, she says, "the one who can rein in her emotions better should do so and stay out of the way of the more dominant person. Also, love must be earned.

Especially with my dad, I was always trying to prove myself to him—whether he was looking or not. I carried this into my marriage almost automatically, constantly bombarding my husband with 'Hey, I did X and Y and Z today!' to justify my existence."

In my case, when my brother died, I tried to be *two* children for my devastated parents in an effort to fill the space he left behind. I tried to heal their grief and their wounds, even though it was a grief that could never be healed. Of course, at age two, I couldn't know that. I didn't think consciously, *I need to heal my parents*. It was just an instinctual response to what I observed and intuited.

But that's when my efforts to buy love began, bending over backward and turning myself inside out for others. As I grew, my parents were very lenient with me, but that provided me with too much risk. There were too many opportunities for experimentation . . . and scary *imperfection*. In order to feel safe, I made my own restrictive rules. My sister came along a few years later, and because she didn't have the same imprinting as I did, she was a born rebel.

When we were in high school, my mother begged the two of us to stay home from school one day so that we could all go to the movies and have lunch together. My sister was on board, but not me. "I *can't*," I said. "I have to go to school!" So my mother and sister went to see *Dirty Dancing*, and I graduated from high school with perfect attendance. Then, as I said, I carried that programming into my marriage.

Can you see from these stories how our relationship beliefs become the director of our relationship story? The good news is that like me, you can decide to retire the old director and take over that job yourself. That's what we're going to do as we continue with this process. Now, let's see what beliefs have been directing *your* life.

Exercise #3: What Beliefs Did You Form as a Result of Your Origin Story?

From the exercises you've completed so far, you ought to have the material necessary to help you discover your relationship beliefs. So refer back to your previous answers when you answer the questions in this exercise.

Bear in mind, though, that beliefs affecting relationships can be formed from any kind of experience. In my case, it wasn't that my parents had the same kind of relationship as the one I ended up with. The imprinting that has affected my relationships the most is related to something else entirely— the death of my brother when I was two. So remember that your relationship beliefs can sometimes have a surprisingly early origin, as well as a surprising influence on your life.

Ask yourself the following questions, and allow the answers to flow without judgment. Don't worry if your answers don't seem to make sense. Beliefs from childhood often don't make logical sense. Even if you don't know exactly what the answers mean right now, you can try to figure them out later.

This is a lengthy journaling session, so give yourself 30 minutes or more to work with the questions. The rewards will be well worth the time spent, so don't put it off!

1. What are the earliest messages you remember receiving about love and relationships as a result of what you heard or observed?

2. If you had both parents at home, what was their relationship like? How did they relate to each other? Were they affectionate and expressive with each other? Were they affectionate and expressive with you?

3. If you had only one parent, what did you come to believe about relationships as a result of the absence of the other parent?

If your parents had romantic relationships separate from each other, what did you make that mean about relationships or yourself? Remember: Even if a parent said nothing about romantic relationships, it's as loud as if they said a lot.

4. If you were raised by your grandparents or other family members, what did you learn about relationships from them? What did you make your family environment mean about relationships and about you?

5. If you were in foster care or adopted, what did you learn about relationships from the adults around you? What did you make foster care or adoption mean about relationships and about you?

6. What kinds of relationships did you see in your family and community? What were the relationships like between grandparents, aunts, uncles, cousins, neighbors, or teachers? What were the dynamics between the adults you observed? Were they contentious, harmonious, unemotional, loving, or confusing?

7. What did you learn about relationships from music, books, television, and movies?

8. Review your answers to the previous questions. Do you see any contradictions or patterns in the messages you received? If so, write them down.

9. What unconscious promises did you make to yourself about relationships? For example, I covertly promised myself that I would be perfect in relationships in order to be

safe and loved. My client Sophia promised herself that she would be a chameleon in relationships because of her belief that no one would love her otherwise.

10. Review your answers again. What conclusions did you make about how relationships work? What beliefs do you think you formed about relationships as a result of these messages? What have you always thought are truisms about romantic relationships?

11. Compare your answers in this exercise to the answers you gave in Exercise #1 in Step 1. Can you now see where some of the stories you've told yourself about relationships came from?

THE TENACITY OF OUR BELIEFS

As you can see, our origin stories give us important clues about the lens through which we view the world. When we're young, we think the world revolves around us, so we feel responsible for everything that happens. Many of us even blame ourselves for events we had no control over, like our parents' divorce or an adult's lack of emotional availability. I thought it was my responsibility to try to heal my parents of a grief that I could scarcely understand. As an adult, it seems silly to think such a thing, but as a two-year-old, I believed my survival depended on it.

We're so impressionable when we're young that these beliefs are practically engraved on our psyches. They're tenacious because we created them to understand how the world works. We had no frame of reference for seeing the world in a different way.

In adulthood, these beliefs often remain unconscious and result in habitual and compulsive behavior. As I've said, they are like the directors of our lives and relationships, but they operate in an almost ghostly way, underneath our awareness. We don't even recognize that we need to uncover them and change them.

Again, one of my beliefs was that no one would take care of me, that I had to do everything myself, and that I'd better not need anything from anyone else. The truth is that my parents took excellent care of me when I was growing up, but my false belief that I wasn't cared for was solidified at such a young age that it stayed with me.

When we become conscious of these beliefs, we often find that they're utterly illogical and nonsensical. Yet if we don't uncover and challenge them in adulthood, we continue to relate to them as facts, and they affect our relationships.

Of course, some of our illogical beliefs are conscious. But we relate to them as though they're logical. For example, some people believe there's no such thing as a happy marriage. Even when presented with objective proof that their belief is false, it's hard for them to release the hold of that ingrained belief. But if you gather a group of people, the beliefs they're holding on to will vary and contradict one another. They can't all be objective facts, right?

Even if we understand intellectually that a belief isn't true, it isn't always easy to release its emotional hold. That's the case for me with my belief that I have to assert my independence. I know it isn't necessary all the time, but emotionally I still sometimes act as if it is. My laziness trigger is another case in point. I *know* I need to cultivate a positive sort of "laziness" in myself, making space for fun and joy and not working so hard all the time. I *know* I need to stop judging people for taking leisure time. But since I was convinced laziness was dangerous when I was young, overcoming this belief is an ongoing process. I have to continue to find my own version of laziness in order to have more compassion for others.

It takes work to challenge and change our false beliefs so that we can replace them with new, true ones that no longer hold us back. As we work toward establishing our *chosen* beliefs in our lives, the old ones will still show up from time to time. So the more we're able to catch ourselves falling prey to the old programming, the more we're able to move forward in a positive way in our relationships with ourselves and others. Balance is always the goal.

Exercise #4: Prove Your Beliefs Wrong

If you read my book Worthy, *you may recognize this exercise. But in this case, you'll explore beliefs about relationships rather than money.*

Part 1—Counter Your Beliefs

Now that you know many of your relationship beliefs, let's see which ones you can prove wrong right now. In Part 2, you'll work on creating a new, empowering belief to replace each of the limiting beliefs.

1. Draw two vertical lines down a piece of paper, or create three columns on your computer screen.

    Label the left-hand column "Old Belief."
    Label the middle column "Counter-Example."
    Label the right-hand column "New Belief."

2. Look at the beliefs you wrote down in Exercise #2 and choose five beliefs that you feel are most negatively impacting you in relationships. Write them in the "Old Belief" column, drawing a horizontal line under each one across all the columns.

Old Belief	Counter-Example	New Belief
1. I have to be perfect in order to be loved in a relationship.		
2.		
3.		
4.		
5.		

3. Next, look at each belief, and ask yourself if there's ever been a counter-example to that belief. Can you remember a time in your life when each of these beliefs was proven untrue? For example, let's say that, like me, you believe that you have to be perfect in order to be loved in a relationship. Can you recall a time when someone loved you for what you deemed an imperfection? Maybe they thought it was cute. Maybe you believe you'll always be betrayed in relationships. Has there been a time when you *weren't* betrayed? If you can't remember a time in your own history,

surely you know others who haven't been betrayed in their romantic relationships. In the middle column next to each belief, write down your counter-example. If you can think of more than one, write them all down!

Old Belief	Counter-Example	New Belief
1. I have to be perfect in order to be loved in a relationship.	My partner has told me he loves parts of my personality that I'm most embarrassed about.	
2.		
3.		
4.		
5.		

4. If you truly can't think of a counter-example for a belief, place a star in the second column. Chances are, by the time you finish the book, you'll be able to go back and fill it in!

Part 2—Create New Beliefs

Next, let's create new beliefs that feel empowering and positive.

Read each belief in the left-hand column again, and create a new belief in the third column on the right. You can often simply choose the opposite belief to the one you're holding. For example, if your belief is "relationships are painful," the new belief might be "relationships are joyful." Play around and try one or two different options before choosing the new belief you like best.

Once you have the column filled out, make a commitment to your new, more empowering beliefs. You might even want to write your new beliefs down and keep them somewhere that you'll see them. Invest in a set of dry-erase markers and write the new beliefs on your mirror, or use sticky notes. (Anyone who has come to my house knows I always keep a jar of markers in the bathroom for just this purpose!) If you're artistic, consider turning your new beliefs into artwork that you can post in a prominent place. The key is to look at them frequently and begin to incorporate them into your consciousness daily, gradually making them your new reality.

Old Belief	Counter-Example	New Belief
1. I have to be perfect in order to be loved in a relationship.	My partner has told me he loves parts of my personality that I'm most embarrassed about.	I'm lovable just as I am.
2.		
3.		
4.		
5.		

Relationship Reframe

"My new, chosen beliefs replace all negative beliefs about relationships that I formed in childhood or in past relationships."

Step 3

Revisit Your Relationship History

When Rhonda got married, she found herself playing out some of the same patterns that her parents had modeled for her. "My dad was always at the bar, and when he came home, my mom would scream and fight with him," she says. "Mom was vicious, and he just took it. Now I can see how I became enraged in my own marriage. My husband is very passive like my dad was. So to get his attention, I used to feel like I had to scream to be heard— just like my mom."

Rhonda has since learned to control her rage. It's easy to see where her pattern came from, but for many of us, tracing our relationship patterns can be more complex.

Michelle's parents, for example, have been married long enough to pass their 50th anniversary. "They've supported each other and built a life together," she says. "They stayed together even when it was hard. The model is that there is this person in your life who is your partner. The alchemy of the two together is greater than the sum of the parts. The relationship creates a foundation of support and intimacy that grows with time, memories, and experiences."

Sounds good, right? But even if our parents model beautiful relationships for us like Michelle's did, we can still walk away with difficult lessons to learn. My parents, for example, have been married for nearly 60 years and have a fantastic relationship. Still, there were other events in our lives that got twisted into negative relationship patterns—none of which mirrored my parents' marriage at all. The same is true for Michelle.

As a result of watching her parents' relationship, she has come to believe that being with someone is better than being alone. By itself, that belief isn't a problem . . . unless the fear of being alone is attached to it. In Michelle's case, add to that a negative image of the "old maid."

"My cousin was never married, and my sister and I always worried about being like her, without considering that she might have been perfectly happy as a single person," Michelle says. Now divorced, Michelle finds it difficult to no longer be part of a couple. "I still get anxious sometimes when I come home and my house is empty and quiet," she says. "I come from the place of the black-and-white, either/or model." When she meets someone new, she's so hopeful that he will be all she's wanted that she often derails the relationship before it gets started. This is a common pattern I see in quite a few of my clients.

What we observe and experience when we're young creates beliefs that create patterns in our relationships. We might find ourselves matched up with people who are much like our father or our mother. Gender doesn't matter. For instance, a straight man might end up in relationships with women who have traits like his father.

Or you might be like me. I hold a belief that creates a relationship pattern very different from what I observed in the adults I grew up around. Since my strongest belief is that "no one will ever take care of me," every single relationship I've had until now has been about rescuing my partner in some way. And the only way I was able to disengage from that pattern was to become aware of it and do the work that I'm outlining for you in these chapters. Thanks to this devoted course of internal work, I no longer experience that particular pattern in my relationship with Aaron.

So the next step is about revisiting your relationship history. As you take a look at relationships throughout your life, you'll begin to "connect the dots" between your origin story, beliefs, and relationship patterns. Actually, rather than dots, let's call them "stars." I think of them as a constellation that illuminates the patterns we want to resolve and dissolve. Once we're aware of these difficult patterns, we have the opportunity to create new ones that align with what we truly want.

Remember: Our beliefs and patterns will stay in place unless we make a concerted effort to change them. If we don't look, the patterns continue—and we stay on the hamster wheel with little hope of progress. As Debbie Ford said, "Our fear of change, our fear of stepping into new realities, is so deep that we desperately cling to the world we know. We often mistake familiarity for safety. The perceived comfort we derive from what is familiar keeps us living in the illusion of our stories." So this step will help you bust that illusion, let go of the safety of familiarity, and step into your truth.

This step often provides the most profound insights for my clients, and it can be emotional. As I cautioned you in the previous chapter, please practice excellent self-care as you go through this process. Show yourself compassion as you recall your past. Leave judgments at the door. Instead, try to look at things objectively, from a place of curiosity rather than self-criticism.

Exercise #5: Draw Your Relationship Timeline

In this exercise, you'll draw a timeline of your romantic relationships. You can start as early as you like, perhaps even in elementary school.

1. On paper or your electronic device, make a list of all the romantic relationships you've had. You don't have to remember the people you dated briefly, but if someone had an impact on you, include them. If you don't remember the person's name, simply make note of something you remember about him/her.

2. For each relationship on your list, write about what happened. You may find it cathartic to write freely about it for several minutes. Just make sure to include each of the following: (a) how you felt in the relationship; (b) how you were treated; (c) the main issues the two of you faced; and (d) how the relationship ended.

    Here's an example. Of course, you can go into much more detail if you feel it's helpful, especially for those relationships that have been particularly important in your life:

    "He was clingy and possessive, always jealous if I even said hello to another guy. I felt suffocated and controlled, but I didn't have the courage to break up with him. He ended up accusing me of cheating on him and left me. Then, even though I'd wanted to break up with him, I felt hurt and abandoned."

3. When you've finished with your timeline, go back and review each entry. Place a star by

the ones that were the most significant. In a few pages, you'll work with these further.

4. Your timeline is, in some ways, a map of your life. It can be painful to review it, so take a moment to appreciate the wisdom of your journey. Wrap your arms around yourself and hold yourself tight for a few moments. Acknowledge your courage as you do this work!

5. Remember: Keep your timeline handy because you'll work with it again later in the chapter.

THOSE PERSISTENT RELATIONSHIP PATTERNS

Often, we feel like we experience the "same thing" from one relationship to the next, even though each time we're sure we've chosen someone very different from our past partners. These are our recurring patterns, and your relationship timeline will help you decipher yours. Bear in mind that sometimes the outward experience from one relationship to another may be different, but what you *feel* is the same—rejected, jealous, put down, suffocated, overwhelmed, etc.

As I said early on in the book, the common denominator in all of your relationships is *you*, which is why changing the pattern starts by going within, not necessarily choosing someone who's different (although that might also be important).

My client Valerie says she has a tendency to attract men who don't care as much about her as she cares about them. This is the "same thing" that happens for her in relationship after relationship.

Maria's "same thing" is men who pursue her and make all sorts of promises to reel her in—but don't see things through, leaving her feeling duped.

Jocelyn has had a similar pattern, and when her partners don't fulfill her needs, she feels disappointed, unheard, and abandoned.

For Eleanor, it's a different experience. "I'm always looking for an out, a reason to end it before they end it with me." Her fear of abandonment is so deep that in her current relationship, she struggles to fully commit. "I'm always watching for signs that the end is coming," she says. This stems from her origin story, which led her to develop the belief that marriage is hurtful and unsafe.

Other common patterns include self-sacrifice or needing to always be right because we fear that being wrong means there's something wrong with us. My own pattern of codependency is very common among my clients, both men and women. I define codependency as looking for someone outside of me to regulate me emotionally. (We'll cover codependency in more detail in Step 8.)

For example, Charles watched his mother always put herself out for others, and it created a similar pattern in his own relationships. He has found women who need him, but aren't necessarily in love with him. "I felt I could always give, and that would make the person happy and make her stay with me." He did eventually get married, but that pattern followed him into his marriage.

Like Charles, we often look for ways to overstep our own boundaries in order to guarantee love. We put aside what we want and need, working instead to make the other person love us, no matter how much we sacrifice ourselves in the process.

Our romantic relationship patterns can even bleed into business situations. Lily came to the realization that her pattern of compromising too much in romantic relationships also played out in her work life. "When I was making jewelry, there were times I created pieces I thought I 'should' create to cater to 'everyone.' Those pieces didn't even come close to selling as quickly as the pieces I put my heart into," she says. "At my day job, I catered to a needy boss who was never pleased. I so wanted to make her happy, but my health suffered. And my son suffered because I worked too much."

Jocelyn's pattern has been to dive into relationships headfirst. "I throw my whole being into it. I feel connection and belonging and a sense that someone gets me. This evolves until I start to draw my self-confidence from the other person, which evolves into giving my power away. I morph into a ball of needs that I'm unable to express. I'm often not even aware of my needs, wants, and desires because I'm so busy pouring my energy out toward the other person. Then I become disappointed that he hasn't met my needs. Yet I haven't asked for what I needed. The cycle amplifies. I then operate from a place of need rather than connection or vulnerability."

Michelle's pattern is to have crushes on men who aren't interested in her, while always finding something wrong with the men who pursue her. She's come to realize that this is a protective mechanism to keep her from being hurt. She's also begun to see that when she rejects men who are interested in her, she's doing the same thing to them that the men she really wants have done to her. It's been an opportunity for her to discover one of her shadow selves—the one who rejects people without giving them a chance. She uncovered another shadow when she realized that she gets upset with men for not honoring their commitments, while she often fails to honor her own commitments to herself.

Anna discovered a shadow self when she realized that her pattern of criticizing her husband for not taking good care of himself physically was a mirror for how she wasn't giving herself the emotional self-care she needed.

Dani also realized that a shadow has played out in her relationships. "I don't stand up for what I want. Then I complain and feel bad for myself because the other person doesn't listen. But the truth is that I'm the one not listening to myself."

Can you relate to any of these stories? Let's work with your timeline further to see if you can uncover more insights.

Bad Boy/Bad Girl Syndrome

When I say "bad boy" or "bad girl," I don't mean it literally. But it's a phrase we're all familiar with, and it's common for both men and women to choose partners who take from them, treat them disrespectfully, love them and leave them, or sometimes even abuse them.

Eleanor says she often participated in relationships with difficult men who needed her to save them. Even though her friends didn't like the guys, she considered herself to be the only person who could understand them. "I was terrible at communicating my needs and kept most feelings inside, but I could always be counted on to abandon myself," she says.

Jocelyn has had a similar pattern and allowed a boyfriend to take money from her. "While spontaneously taking a road trip to Atlantic City and gambling all night, I withdrew $500 from my checking account to give to him. I couldn't find the words to say, 'No, I'm not comfortable giving you that amount of money. No, you don't have the money to repay me, and I don't trust you'll ever repay me.' I'm so uncomfortable with conflict that I've dimmed my own light," she says. She eventually married this man. During the months before the wedding, she had terrible eczema, which she now believes was a warning from her soul—a message she didn't listen to. When he moved into her apartment, she didn't ask him to split expenses. "I allowed him to sponge off me and didn't have the courage to stick up for myself. I was already paying all the expenses and convinced myself it was okay that he didn't contribute. I dismissed the voices that told me of his affairs. I made the choice to look away, rather than to speak up or create conflict."

Leah says that in the past she thought as long as she complied with what her boyfriend wanted, she'd be able to change his bad-boy qualities and turn him into a better man. "Being a savior meant I was doing something valuable and would be more loved for it," she says. "Bad boys seemed to live more fiercely and add more excitement to the life I grew up in. But they also were the dominant force in the relationships, and I ended up being the doormat. The men I dated would always be critical, and I'd just take it, leading to physical or emotional abuse because I had no self-worth. One man left me shattered because he told me he was moving on to someone better—prettier, thinner, smarter, and with more money."

While the "bad boy" syndrome is more common, there are plenty of men who also have the "bad girl" or "damsel in distress" syndrome. Men with this pattern often play the role of the "knight in shining armor," always coming to the rescue of a woman who takes advantage of them.

Is this a pattern in your own relationship history? If so, it's an indication that you need to work on self-love. The more you learn to love yourself, the less likely you'll allow someone to take advantage of you.

Exercise #6: Discover Your Relationship Patterns

In this exercise, you'll begin the "connecting the dots/stars" process. This is in-depth, so block out as much time as you can—a full hour if you can swing it. You may need to spend a few days with this exercise before you're able to answer all the questions for each important relationship. But please take the necessary time because the insights you gain will be invaluable.

1. Refer to your Relationship Timeline, and create a new column or list next to the most significant relationships. (You may choose to do this exercise for the entire list, but if not, at least complete it for the most important relationships in your history.) In this column, ask yourself the following questions about each relationship:

   a. What choices did I make in this re-lationship?

   b. Did I tolerate something that was less than loving to myself?

   c. Did I sabotage myself or the relationship?

   d. Did I ask for what I wanted, or did I hide my true feelings?

   e. Did I give more than I received?

   f. Did I take more than I gave?

   g. Did I withhold love or intimacy?

   h. Did I cause my partner suffering?

   i. Was there conflict? If so, did I initiate the conflict, or did I cower from conflict? Or was there an uncomfortable absence of conflict even though there was tension in the air?

j.   What were my emotional triggers in this relationship?

k.   What qualities or behaviors in my partner did I find abhorrent that I now realize I possess or exhibit myself?

Here's an example:

a.   What choices did I make in this relationship? *I chose to stay even though I was put down and not treated with respect.*

b.   Did I tolerate something that was less than loving to myself? *Yes, I tolerated verbal cruelty and lack of respect.*

c.   Did I sabotage myself or the relationship? *Yes, I sabotaged myself by not feeling worthy enough to leave when I wasn't given the care and respect I deserved.*

d.   Did I ask for what I wanted, or did I hide my true feelings? *I never asked for what I really wanted, and I hid many of my true feelings because I was afraid of losing my partner's love.*

e.   Did I give more than I received? *Yes, I thought if I continued to give, he would change, but the more I gave, the less he seemed to respect me.*

f.   Did I take more than I gave? *No, I don't think so.*

g.   Did I withhold love or intimacy? *I didn't think so at the time. But looking back, I see I hid a lot of my true self out of the fear of not being loved, so in that respect, I see that I withheld true intimacy.*

h. Did I cause my partner suffering? *I thought I had the one time I allowed myself to get angry, but now I realize I was just standing up for myself. My inability to be authentic may have caused him suffering.*

i. Was there conflict? Did I initiate conflicts, or did I cower from conflict? Or was there an uncomfortable absence of conflict even though there was tension in the air? *There was a lot of conflict, and I retreated from it except for the one time I spoke up. He seemed to lose his temper no matter what I did. I couldn't do anything right in his eyes.*

j. What were my emotional triggers in this relationship? *I was triggered by his temper, which made me cower like I did as a child when my parents got mad. I felt angry when he acted in a way that reminded me of my mom, but I only dared express my anger once. Then I felt guilty about it.*

k. What qualities or behaviors in my partner did I find abhorrent that I now realize I possess or exhibit myself? *Definitely the anger. I hated his anger, but I had a lot of my own anger that was pent up and unexpressed. In some ways, I think he was expressing what I couldn't. Plus, he mirrored my inner voice when he put me down and was disrespectful to me. My inner critic also put me down, and I was disrespectful to myself because I allowed his treatment of me to continue.*

2. After you've answered all of these questions for each of your important relationships, go

back through and reread them, looking for patterns. For example, have you sabotaged yourself repeatedly? Have you cowered from conflict or initiated conflict? Have you consistently hidden your true self or parts of yourself from your partners? Ask yourself these questions:

a. What experiences have happened repeatedly, across multiple relationships?

b. What traits or behaviors have shown up in my partners over and over, and what shadows do these indicate within me?

c. In what ways have I been triggered in my relationships? Is there a pattern here?

d. How have I felt in my relationships? If those feelings have been the same in many relationships, can I now see that those feelings came from inside me rather than anything the other person did or didn't do?

e. Note if my patterns changed at any point in my history. If so, were the new patterns better or worse? Can I pinpoint what happened to bring about the change?

3. Take written note of everything you discovered. Don't count on your memory! These kinds of emotional insights can be fleeting because the part of us that's afraid wants us to forget them. Don't allow that to happen. Write your answers down so you can refer to them again and again. This will help you to make changes and create the kind of relationship you desire. You deserve

nothing less, so writing it all down will turn you into your own rescuer. That sounds good, right?

UNDERLYING COMMITMENTS

As you step into new levels of insight and awareness, I want to introduce you to one of the most powerful concepts for me personally and for my clients—"underlying commitments," which was coined by Debbie Ford. The truth is that we're completely capable of creating what we're most committed to. The problem is that what we *think* or *say* we're committed to is often at odds with another commitment held in our unconscious mind. In other words, we believe we're committed to one thing, but we're actually—subconsciously—committed to something else. Whenever there's a discrepancy between what we say we want and what we're actually experiencing, it's due to an underlying commitment—a stronger commitment in the unconscious that was made out of fear, which will override any other desires we have. For example, I might say that I want to be seen and heard, but I'm more committed to staying invisible and silent because that's what feels safe to me.

Underlying commitments are the result of our limiting beliefs. We create them as coping mechanisms when we're very young, believing they're necessary for our survival. They're our *first* and *strongest* commitments, because they were formed when we were young, vulnerable, and impressionable.

We aren't aware of them because they're in the shadows of the unconscious, but our relationship patterns are their outward manifestation. Until we become aware of these commitments and make new, *conscious* commitments, it's difficult to change our patterns. In fact, if you're stuck in a relationship pattern, you can be sure it's due to an underlying commitment.

These commitments are fueled by the limiting beliefs we covered in Step 2. If you have a belief that you're unlovable, for example, you might make an unconscious commitment to yourself about how to be in the world based on that belief. Maybe your commitment is to make sure you don't get hurt, for example. Then, with this underlying commitment installed in your unconscious, you will keep that promise to yourself no matter how much you *say* you want a relationship. You might find partners who don't really love you, or you don't believe it when partners tell you they love you. Or you might end relationships prematurely to beat your partners to the rejection that you're sure is inevitable. First and foremost, you're going to make sure you don't get hurt.

Other common underlying commitments include: staying safe, being invisible, staying silent, being independent and self-sufficient, not wanting to be controlled, or not feeling happy. We hold to these commitments out of a need for safety. We think we're sparing ourselves pain, but often we cause ourselves even more pain. Why, for example, would someone have an underlying commitment to *not* feeling happy? Only because they hold the false belief that happiness is not a safe emotion to have.

How do these underlying commitments play out? Let's look at what some of my clients discovered when doing the exercises in this chapter.

Grace says her underlying commitment has been to keep her heart protected by maintaining control over strong feelings of love and joy. As a result, in her relationships, she has withheld her love for the sake of safety—while still expecting love from her partner. She's felt like a victim, believing that she's been deprived of a close, intimate bond. But she now understands that she's been afraid of intimacy and has had a lifelong commitment to keeping it at a distance. Knowing this, she can practice becoming more comfortable with intimacy and expressions of love.

Leah has discovered that one of her underlying commitments is to avoid a relationship unless everything is "perfect"—she's perfect, her partner is perfect, and the relationship itself is perfect. This has caused her to try to mold her partners into the fantasy man in her mind. At the same time, one of her beliefs has been that she'll never be happy in a relationship because to do so would mean losing her power. Since she's unconsciously committed to not losing her power, she can't allow a relationship to flourish—it's simply too dangerous. "While I kept telling myself I wanted a loving relationship with the right man, I was unconsciously committed to remaining single in order to not feel more pain," she says. This is a good example of how we can have underlying commitments that fight against each other. Remember that we develop these before we have adult logic in place!

Anna says that when she was a child, she felt she had to stay quiet and submissive in order to be loved. So she made the commitment to stay quiet in order to fit in. "But the irony is that I never felt like I fit in, because I couldn't express myself," she says.

She also didn't see much of a connection between her parents, so she's stayed more committed to having time and space alone than to creating a deeply intimate relationship with her husband. This is one of the reasons she's felt the need to "do it all" around the house. "I never really got the concept of partnership until I met my husband," she says. "I did everything. We'd come home from the grocery store and I'd literally grab all the bags. He'd be standing there holding the keys, teasing me, 'You wanna get the door, too?' I believed that my needs wouldn't get met if I asked for help, so I didn't ask. Yet, the irony was, I unconsciously played the role of the victim as a result. 'Poor me. Nobody helps me.'"

One of her underlying commitments might be to simply maintain her belief so that she can feel like a martyr. The martyr role can help us feel secure and important. It can feed self-esteem in a false way, while actually robbing us of self-love. This is a common pattern for many of us (myself included!). But the more we begin to care for ourselves—to genuinely care about our own feelings, needs, and desires—the more we're able to accept help and love from others. At the same time, we stop feeling like we have to buy love from others.

Let's see if we can bring some of your own underlying commitments into your awareness.

Exercise #7: Excavate Your Underlying Commitments

This exercise will help you begin to excavate your underlying commitments. Even though you aren't getting what you want in relationships, what you're receiving is actually in perfect alignment with what you've been most committed to on the level of the unconscious.

This is another in-depth exercise, and it might take time to figure these commitments out. So be patient. But since this exercise is in four parts—to give you different ways to ask the questions—you might be surprised by some of your answers.

Part 1—"I Say I Want" Sentences

1. Complete the following sentence as many
    times as necessary to express all the ways in
    which your relationships have disappointed
    you. Refer back to your Relationship
    Timeline to help you. To jog your memory,
    you might also want to review your answers
    to Exercise #1 in Step 1.

    "I say I want _____,

    _____

    but what I'm experiencing is _____

    _____."

    Here are some examples:
    "I say I want a loving relationship, but what
    I'm experiencing is men who always leave me."
    "I say I want deep intimacy with my wife,
    but what I'm experiencing is a lack of closeness
    and connection between us."
    "I say I want to be treated with respect by
    my husband, but what I'm experiencing is a lack
    of consideration for my feelings."

2. Make a list of the actions, habits, patterns,
    and choices you see in yourself that are
    inconsistent with what you say you desire.
    What choices have you made that take you
    away from achieving what you say you want?
    Again, refer to your Relationship Timeline as
    necessary.

3. Imagine that there is an underlying
    commitment that's causing you to make
    these choices and take these actions. If those

choices and actions were a direct reflection of some unseen commitment you've held, what do you imagine that commitment would be? In other words, what would a person have to be committed to in order to behave this way?

Example #1:

What I say and experience: *I say I want a loving relationship, but what I'm experiencing is men who always leave me.*

Actions, choices, habits: *I tend to dismiss men who appear stable, assuming they're "boring" before I give them a chance.*

Possible underlying commitment: *A person experiencing this would have to be committed to being alone.*

Example #2:

What I say and experience: *I say I want deep intimacy with my wife, but what I'm experiencing is a lack of closeness and connection between us.*

Actions, choices, habits: *I fear intimacy and don't really let my wife in or make an effort to get closer to her.*

Possible underlying commitment: *A person experiencing this would have to be committed to staying safe within himself, not allowing anyone to get too close out of fear that he's unlovable.*

4. Now reread your answers to #3. Does this underlying commitment ring true for you? Why do you think you made this commitment?

Example: If I'm committed to being alone, why might that be the case? What am I afraid will happen if I'm in a relationship? I think I'm afraid of both being hurt and losing my sense of autonomy.

Part 2—Your Underlying Commitments

Refer back to the beliefs you wrote down in Exercise #3 in Step 2 on page 27. For each one, ask yourself this question: What's the likely underlying commitment that someone with this belief would hold?

Example: My belief is that I'm not worthy if I don't take care of everyone else's needs. Someone with that belief probably has an underlying commitment to making sure they're loved through "earning" their worth.

Part 3—New Commitments

1. Choose your most potent underlying commitment, and write a new belief and new commitment that declares what you truly want.

    Example: Underlying commitment: To be alone so that I can be free since I don't believe I can be free in a relationship.

    New belief: I can be free even while in a relationship.

    New commitment: I'm committed to being in a romantic partnership that allows us both to be free.

2. Next, ask yourself what you'll have to give up in order to make this new commitment.

    Example: To be in a romantic partnership that allows us both to be free, I'll have to give up

*my belief that relationships rob us of freedom.
I'll have to give up being a victim.*

3. Finally, think of one small action you can take to begin to adopt your new commitment.

   Examples: Three times a week, I'll visualize the new kind of free relationship I want.

   OR: I'll write my new belief and new commitment several times a day and put them on the wall where I can see them repeatedly.

   OR: I'll put something in my pocket or on my phone to remind me to remember my new belief and commitment throughout the day.

   OR: All of the above!

4. Imagine how your life will be different with this new commitment in place. What will change, especially with regard to your relationships? Write down what you envision.

Part 4—Your Inner Child

Take a moment to open your heart and give compassion to your inner child, who created these underlying commitments from a place of self-preservation. Honor the child's fear, and make peace with these old commitments. Let your inner child know that you no longer need these old commitments and that you're adopting new ones. Affirm that you'll continue to take care of your inner child.

Relationship Reframe

"I release old, dysfunctional relationship patterns
and underlying commitments, and I commit
to freely loving myself and others."

Step 4

Make Peace with Your Past . . . and Let It Go

When relationships end, there's a lot to grieve—more than just the loss of that person. There are your mutual friends, his/her family, the objects you shared, your home, and even the inside jokes. There's no graveyard for such things.

I was unexpectedly distraught, for example, when I decided to get rid of the land line my ex-husband and I shared. It had been our phone number for such a long time. Later, when a comedian we both loved died, a part of me wanted to share that loss with him . . . but I couldn't.

The worst was when our dog passed away. The divorce agreement with my ex stated there would be no direct contact between us. So one day, a mutual friend received a text from him asking that I be told our dog had a tumor on his heart and had only a few days left. Sure enough, two days later, I got word from another friend that our dog had died. It had been nearly six years since I'd seen the dog or my ex-husband.

Leaving my dog was one of the most painful aspects of my divorce. To accept that I couldn't bring the dog with me, I had to grieve him as if he had already died. But when I got the news that he had actually passed, it felt like he died "all over again." I was flooded with memory upon memory. For my ex and me, the dog had been our last link to one another.

As a result, I found myself feeling grief again for what was, what wasn't, and what would never be. Grief for who we'd been and who we couldn't be. Grief I had thought I'd left behind years before.

I was with my ex for 18 years, so yes, feelings still come up. Sometimes it's like a sucker punch to the gut. I'll be reminded of some aspect of our marriage out of the blue, and it will take me right back into the throes of the emotions.

This is why I don't really believe in "closure." It's one of those buzzwords that those of us in the self-development field like to use. We want to put the final period on the past and move on. And I agree it's important to let the past go. *But* I don't really believe there is such a thing as 100 percent closure. Growth isn't linear, after all, and our issues are multilayered. Many teachers speak of growth as a spiral. This means that our issues come back around from time to time. We might work on an issue and believe we've let it go, but then, seemingly out of nowhere, there it is again. For many of us, it can be an excuse to beat ourselves up. We must not have done it right the first time, or we didn't let go "enough." But that isn't necessarily the case.

When issues we've worked on consciously come back, it's most often because a new layer or level of that issue needs to be addressed. This time, it's a graduate-level course, whereas last time around it was 101. But I don't believe we ever "arrive" at some final state of enlightenment, at least not while we're in a body on this planet.

The human condition is what it is. In my opinion, if we're here, we're still a work in progress.

When it comes to the most impactful relationships in our lives, in my experience true and final closure doesn't happen. Every time I see my ex-husband superimposed on Aaron, I have to make the choice again to let that old relationship go. I have the choice to feel hijacked, angry, and fearful, or I can choose to feel accepting and grateful.

With that choice, closure has become more of a "finding peace practice" for me. When the emotions or issues revisit me, I breathe and choose peace. It's less about no longer being affected by the past than it is about having a shorter recovery time from the inevitable sucker punch.

So that's what Step 4 is all about—making peace with your past and letting it go . . . with the caveat that letting go is an ongoing practice. Just remember: There's no race to make peace. There's no benefit to avoiding the work, but there's also no benefit to rushing yourself through it.

WE CAN ONLY RELEASE WHAT'S FIRMLY IN OUR GRASP

Have you ever heard a friend insist, "I'm totally over it! Really—I've completely let that go and am ready to move on to bigger and better things in my life." Meanwhile, you can feel their trigger right under the surface? Maybe their jaw is so tight that their teeth are almost clenched. Clearly they *want* to be over it, but the anger and hurt are still churning below like a volcano waiting to erupt. We've all been there, right?

Often we want to rush to let go of the past without having allowed our emotions their moment in the sun. We try to bypass the hard part, which is feeling the pain, in an effort to speed up the healing process. But it never works. We can't release something that isn't firmly in our grasp. Before we can make peace with someone or a difficult event, we have to *lean into* the feelings.

Yes, I know, that's the last thing any of us wants to do. But it's the only way to achieve peace. We have to invite ourselves to really feel the pain. As I've mentioned in previous chapters, that might mean punching a pillow or crying hard. And as I've also said, you might have to do that multiple times. Plus, the pain might revisit you on the growth spiral years from now. The key is to allow the feelings to flow when they rise to the surface. If they don't flow, they can't release.

If you find it difficult to bring your emotions to the surface, I suggest paying attention to what you do to avoid your feelings. Some of us go for food, some of us turn on the TV, and some of us exercise or go shopping. The next time you feel compelled to engage in one of these avoidance strategies, ask yourself, "What am I feeling right now?" Sit down and be silent for a few minutes, or begin to write in your journal without thinking about what you're writing. Just allow any words to flow whether you think they make sense or not. This is a way the unconscious mind can surprise us with what we're hiding from ourselves.

For some of us, connecting with our emotions is a difficult process, and it might take some work with a therapist to unearth them. But the bottom line is that you can't heal what you can't feel!

Here's an example from my own life of feeling the feelings so that I could move on. A few years ago, my ex was living in a condo, and per our divorce agreement, I was obligated to pay the mortgage. But then, that obligation expired. Since the loan was in my name, he just assumed I'd continue paying it because it's exactly what

I'd have done in the past. He was relating to me as if I were the same woman I'd been in our marriage—scared to death of ruining her credit and willing to bail him out no matter what.

Stopping the payments meant my credit score had to take a hit, but my self-love and self-respect were more important. I was no longer the woman who needed to buy his love or have perfect credit.

Still, I had to shift my thinking and emotions to resist the urge to fall back into my old patterns. I had to invite myself to *lean in* to the feelings I had about it. A part of me still held the belief that my ex couldn't survive without me. So I had to let myself feel my fears that he wouldn't be okay and that he'd blame me for his problems. That was the only way I could let go of more of my sense of responsibility for him. (Notice I said "more" rather than "all." I'm fully prepared for the possibility that these feelings could come back up to the surface at some point.)

I also had to feel the anger inside me. Why wasn't he stepping up and paying the mortgage like an adult? Why wasn't he willing to take responsibility for his own life? Why was he still counting on me to bail him out?

Once I allowed myself to feel all of those feelings, and I talked myself through the wisdom of my new resolve, I felt confident about my choice to stop paying the mortgage.

The process I went through had many steps that I'll invite you to explore in the next exercise: (1) I allowed myself to air my grievances toward my ex—not to him personally, but in my journal; (2) I felt the hurt, pain, fear, and vulnerability about this issue with him; and (3) I acknowledged my own part in the situation and how throughout our marriage I habitually gave to him out of a place of fear and habit.

Let's see what comes up for you as you work through this first part of the letting-go process.

Exercise #8: Air Your Grievances

This exercise consists of two parts. It isn't about airing your grievances directly to the person involved. It's between you and you—an inner exploration and releasing process. If you're in a relationship with someone now, I urge you to pause on sharing your grievances at the moment. In the next chapter, we'll talk about how to communicate issues to one another. But for now, just work within yourself.

Be sure to store the pages in a safe place where your partner isn't going to stumble upon them. This exercise should be for your eyes only, unless you want to share it with a close friend, therapist, or coach.

Part 1—"Air Out" Your Past Relationships

1. Take a look at the relationship history you created in the previous step. For the relationships that have the most emotional charge, write down your complaints and resentments about each: *I'm angry with [insert name] because* _____

   _____ .

   Then write freely about what happened and how you felt.

   Example: I'm angry with Marsha because she blamed me for everything in our relationship without ever taking responsibility for her part in it.

2. Next, write about how this resentment has affected you. Did it affect your self-esteem? Did it activate fears? Did it cause you to feel less trusting and hide yourself more?

   Example: This resentment has affected my self-esteem, making me feel like I was to blame for everything that went wrong between us. It also made me defensive, so that I'd get emotionally triggered by future partners whenever I was blamed for something.

3. Now that you've identified your feelings about each grievance, write a note to the person involved. Pull out all the stops, putting aside your spiritual wisdom for the moment. Get your anger out on the page, and let yourself blame them all you want. (If you have several relationships you want to work on, you can do this gradually. Just don't put it off for too long. If you can, complete all of them within a week, or two weeks maximum.)

   Example: Dan, I was crushed when you left me. You didn't even seem to care how much it hurt me. You just walked away as if I didn't matter at all. You were heartless. It left me feeling so small and unimportant, like I wasn't worth anything. I also felt stupid for having stayed with someone who had so little empathy for others.

Part 2—Take Responsibility for Your Past Relationships

1. Now it's time to put your spiritual wisdom hat back on. Think about what part you played in what happened (or is happening) in the relationship. What mistakes did you

make? Were you hurtful, withholding, or dishonest? Did you fail to set appropriate boundaries?

Example: I didn't set boundaries with Dan. I allowed him to always have his way, putting my own needs and wants aside in order to keep the peace and earn his love. In that way, I was both withholding and dishonest with him.

2.   In the previous chapter, you explored some of your shadow selves in each relationship. Has this exercise brought to mind other parts of you that you weren't aware of before? Bear in mind that these can be parts you perceive as "positive" or "negative." For example, you might discover a playful side of you that you didn't know you had.

Example: Dan's selfishness was definitely a shadow for me. I didn't believe I had the right to be selfish or assert my own desires. It was always about making him happy with little thought of my own happiness.

3.   How would you have behaved differently in this relationship if you knew then what you know now? In what way do you wish you had been more thoughtful, compassionate, accepting, and kind in this relationship?

Example: Today, if I were in relationship with Dan, I'd ask for what I want. I sometimes wonder if he left because he got bored with me since I wasn't a whole person in the relationship. Now I'd be more honest with him. I'd understand how my people-pleasing could deprive him of the kind of partner I'm capable of being—a whole, authentic person.

4. If you feel that amends are due to your partner (former or otherwise), write down your apology. Note that it doesn't matter if your partner ever makes amends to you. That's their business; this book and this exercise are for you. You're certainly free to apologize directly to anyone in your life if you want, but for the purposes of this exercise, your amends are for your own healing process.

   Example: Dan, I'm sorry for not bringing my whole self into our relationship and allowing you to see all of me because I was afraid I'd lose your love. Even if the ending had been the same, I wish I had given us a chance to be in a full partnership.

5. If this isn't your current relationship, say good-bye to this person: "Good-bye, [insert name]. I'm leaving this relationship in the past and taking what I've learned with me. I wish you a good and fulfilling life." Of course, add to it whatever feels right to you.

   Example: Good-bye, Dan. I'm leaving this relationship in the past and taking what I've learned with me. I wish you a good and fulfilling life. I'm still working through my anger toward you, but that's okay.

6. Finally, acknowledge yourself with gratitude for going through this process, feeling your emotions, and being honest with yourself. Then, shred or burn what you've written.

PRACTICE FORGIVENESS

As I said at the beginning of the chapter, making peace with the past is a practice, not an achievement. The same can be said for forgiveness. We forgive in bits and pieces; it isn't a finite destination or a total resolution. Again, it's about recovering more quickly each time we have a triggering memory or experience.

So it's important not to rush to forgiveness. We can't gloss over it. That's why we aired our grievances first. We have to walk through our anger before we can consider forgiveness. Remember that we can't release what isn't firmly in our grasp!

Many people try to talk themselves into forgiveness because they believe they "should" forgive. But forgiveness isn't an intellectual exercise. It happens in the heart, which has to melt a bit to surrender to the experience of forgiving.

As my teacher Debbie Ford shared in her book *Spiritual Divorce*, "Forgiveness is the essential component to freeing our hearts and liberating our souls. Forgiveness is the food that nourishes our bodies, our relationships, and our future. Forgiveness is the greatest act of courage because it breaks down the walls that we thought would protect us. Our resentments are like a steel cord wrapped around our past, forever binding us to those we see as our opponents. We must become willing to step through the constricting door of blame into the unbounded world of forgiveness. Forgiveness is the hallway between your past and your future. If you choose to hold on to your anger and resentments, you will continue living a life from your past. What you can always expect when you live a life from your past is more of the same. But if you dare to walk through the door of forgiveness, you will step into a new room and a new reality. You will create a life filled with love, compassion, and passion for living. You'll be ready to create a future based on what you want instead of one created by what you don't want."

To truly forgive and let go of the past, we must also be willing to forgive ourselves. Self-forgiveness can feel strange to those of us who are used to judging ourselves, but when we withhold self-forgiveness, we withhold self-love and self-acceptance. We chastise ourselves for our humanness, as if we aren't lovable unless we're perfect. That leaves us at a deficit in our relationships and in life.

Self-forgiveness practice is a crucial step if we want fulfilling relationships and a fulfilling life. It usually requires even more of a regular practice than forgiving others because most of us are much harder on ourselves.

It's easy to forget and fall into old habits of judging yourself. So when you catch yourself in self-judgment, try this: Take a deep breath, and say aloud or in your mind, "I give myself permission to forgive myself." This may start out as an intellectual process, but as you allow yourself to forgive, your heart will begin to soften.

I also suggest becoming more aware of your inner critic. That negative voice is automatic for most of us, but as you notice it more and more, you can counteract it by taking that deep breath and giving yourself permission to forgive.

In a moment, you'll work through a two-part forgiveness exercise that I adapted from Debbie Ford's powerful work (with the permission of her estate). But for a regular forgiveness practice, you might want to adopt a couple of my clients' ideas.

Andrea has created an altar to her past loves. She places objects on the altar that remind her of what she's gained as a result of knowing them. Then, she regularly lights a candle and uses an adaptation of the Hawaiian practice of reconciliation and forgiveness called Ho'opo-nopono, saying, "I'm sorry. Please forgive me. Thank you. I love you." You can also say those words to yourself for self-forgiveness practice.

Brenda has created a loving-kindness practice toward her ex-husband during her regular meditation, which she says has been exceptionally freeing. Each time, she says, "Despite the hurt, I believe he did the best he could. I believe we each do the best we can in every moment. And when we know better, we do better." This practice serves the dual purpose of forgiving herself *and* someone else.

This is the ultimate way to make peace with your past. Can you imagine a future version of you with more forgiveness for yourself, your past partners, and your current or future partner? Just remember that forgiveness is a practice, not a destination. But you can achieve a strong sense of peace in your life by working through the exercise that follows.

Gratitude

Gratitude is another important part of your forgiveness practice. It can be difficult to feel grateful for something that was painful, but life is about growth. One of the realities of the human experience is that growth often comes with pain.

Garth Brooks wrote a song many years ago called "Unanswered Prayers" about running into an old girlfriend. When he sees her, he remembers how he thought his life was over when they split up. But if they hadn't split, he never would have met his current wife. Usually, when we suffer a loss, there's something better waiting on the horizon. As Paulo Coelho said, "If you're brave enough to say good-bye, life will reward you with a new hello."

That's certainly the way it turned out for me. There's no denying that if my husband hadn't read my journals that fateful day and found out about my affair, you wouldn't be reading this book right now. I wouldn't be coaching people and leading this fulfilling life that has resulted from that experience. I'm sure I'd still be in the marriage, continuing to live out my dysfunctional patterns.

Today I feel gratitude toward my ex-husband for what he and our relationship taught me. It doesn't mean I approve of his behavior, but it means that I see the blessings in my past experiences, no matter how difficult they may have been.

Exercise #9: Forgiveness Practice

This exercise contains two separate meditations as Part 1 and Part 2. The first is a process for forgiving others, while the second is a process for self-forgiveness. Please set aside at least 45 minutes for each of these meditations so you don't rush through them. It would be easy to skip over these, but you'll only get out of this process what you put into it. So I urge you to give yourself this time.

Be sure to turn off all phones so that you can surrender to this process. Wear comfortable clothes, and sit on a comfortable chair or couch. Feel free to play soft music or light candles, if you like. It helps to record your own voice reading the steps so that you don't have to open your eyes, which will disrupt your meditative state. While recording, you can skip the parts of the meditation that are in italics.

Part 1—Meditation for Forgiveness of Others

1. Close your eyes, and take several breaths. Relax each part of your body, starting with your feet. Then, gradually move up your legs, hips, belly, chest, back, arms, neck, and head until you feel fully relaxed. *Don't work too hard at this. Just ask your body to relax. As you continue, it will relax more and more.*

2. Take some deep, slow breaths, using your breath to connect with your heart to the best of your ability. Choose one of the partners from your relationship history that you most need to forgive. Allow yourself to feel the grudge, blame, or resentment you're still carrying toward this person.

3. Imagine that you now have the ability to view this situation through different eyes—to see it in the greater context of your soul's evolution. Ask yourself: "What's the cost in my life of holding on to this blame and resentment? How does this unhealed, unforgiven incident prevent me from having more peace, freedom, and expression?"

4. Take a deep breath and ask yourself: "What is the gift, lesson, or life wisdom that this experience was meant to deliver to me? How will I be able to advance in my life and spiritual journey if I choose to forgive and let go of this blame or resentment?"

5. Take another deep breath, and imagine that you're breathing in the energy of unconditional love and forgiveness. As you exhale, let go of the blame or resentment that you've held on to. Keep inhaling and exhaling until you feel that all the

resentment has been released. If you feel there's too much to release all of it now, that's fine. Let go of what you can for now, and come back to this meditation again and again to release more of it.

6. What can you do to support this process of forgiveness that you've started? Is there some practice or internal focused action you can take to assist you in letting go of this resentment? What specifically do you need to do to encourage forgiveness in your life?

7. When you're ready, open your eyes and write down your answers to the questions in the previous step, including the action(s) you'll take to further let go of this resentment and encourage forgiveness on a day-to-day basis.

Part 2—Meditation for Forgiveness of Self

You can do this immediately after the meditation in Part 1, or you can choose to do this meditation another day. Just don't put it off so long that you forget about it!

1. Close your eyes, and take several breaths. Relax each part of your body, starting with your feet. Then, gradually move up your legs, hips, belly, chest, back, arms, neck, and head until you feel fully relaxed. *Don't work too hard at this. Just ask your body to relax. As you continue, it will relax more and more.*

2. Take some deep, slow breaths, using your breath to connect with your heart to the best of your ability. Then, begin to reflect on the incidents and circumstances from your life that still weigh you down with guilt, shame, remorse, or regret.

3. Allow yourself to answer the following question: "What do I most need to be forgiven for?"

4. Next, reflect on how your life would be different if you no longer felt the burden of this guilt, resentment, regret, or shame. Imagine your day-to-day life without it.

5. Place your hand on your heart, breathe deeply, and consciously say, "I forgive myself for _____ . . ." You can do this for as many issues as you like.

6. Finally, say to yourself aloud or silently, "I relinquish this guilt, resentment, regret, and shame. It was part of my past, and today I'm a new person starting fresh."

7. Give yourself gratitude, and acknowledge yourself for completing this process.

8. Open your eyes, and write down any notes you want to remember. You might wish to add to your forgiveness actions from Part 1 to make self-forgiveness part of your everyday process of bringing more forgiveness into your life.

Relationship Reframe

"I make peace with my past through an ongoing practice of forgiving my former relationship partners, as well as myself."

Step 5

Redefine Intimacy

When you use the word *intimacy*, how do you define it? Does your mind immediately jump to sex? A lot of people define intimacy that way—as closeness that's purely physical. But sex can actually be one of the *least* intimate things we do. We can easily hide our true selves in favor of a solely physical experience, in which we cut ourselves off from our emotions.

Obviously the best sex includes an emotional connection, but true intimacy involves so much more than just taking off our clothes. It includes *emotional* closeness, sharing, collaborative insight, revelation, and authenticity. Most important, it requires honesty and vulnerability.

Most of us say we want more closeness in our relationships, but we don't know how to make that happen. The truth is that we usually stand in our own way. I'm a case in point. For most of my marriage, I was the opposite of intimate. Instead, I kept myself hidden. I kept the secret about my affair, and I hid my true feelings from my husband. I also hid my feelings and relationship issues from everyone else I knew. People thought they knew me, but I only allowed them to know the version of me I chose to show.

Why? Deep shame. The early programming that told me I had to be perfect meant I couldn't let anyone see the chinks in my armor. Unconsciously, I believed it would be the end of me if anybody knew the truth. I didn't just fear losing the love of the people close to me; I feared being rejected and shunned by the world at large.

Many of my clients have found themselves similarly paralyzed by their shame. One client took 10 sessions to admit to me that she'd had an affair, even though her coaching goal was to express herself more and become comfortable in her own skin. It took all of that time for her to reveal her shame. To her credit, she was finally able to do it, and the result was life-changing for her.

As we've already established, fears and beliefs from our childhood tell us we have to hide our true selves. These beliefs are far from rational, but until we become aware of them, they continue to play out that irrationality in our lives. And they usually lead us to create exactly what we don't want.

We think, *I have to hide parts of myself in order to be loved*, when actually, the opposite is true. It may be counterintuitive, but the only way we can experience real love is by revealing ourselves. Hindu Master Sri Prem Baba put it this way: "Often we remain isolated even while relating on various levels. This happens because we have pages in the book of our lives that we don't want to reveal to anyone, not even to ourselves. In this case, fear in the form of shame becomes a barrier that prevents us from growing deeper in any relationship."

My client Leah says the masks she wears to hide her true self became a performance that made her feel "like a trained seal."

"If I'm a chameleon with each person, I have to remember which mask and role I'm playing with each one," she says. "It's like telling a lie. I have to remember the lie and who I told. Then, as time goes by, I can't remember which persona I've played with whom. When the truth of me or another persona comes out, I create mistrust, which is what I wanted to avoid in the first place."

Far too many relationships function on pretense. Each person determines what they think their partner wants, and they try to live up to that image in the hope of being loved. But neither person actually *feels* loved, because whatever love they receive is directed toward the false image, not the true self.

Our greatest longing is to be loved for who we really are. But how can we feel loved if we *hide* who we are? It's so easy to point the finger of blame at the other person and say, "You don't get me!" But if we aren't being honest and open, how can they possibly "get us"?

We all judge parts of ourselves as unacceptable, and the idea of revealing those to someone else can be terrifying. But when we conceal so much of ourselves, we fail to give anyone a chance to love us for our best and our worst. Staying hidden just isn't sustainable in a long-term, committed relationship, at least not if the relationship is meant to be based on true intimacy. The closeness and connection we want so much will continue to elude us until we consciously step into the scary territory of revealing more of ourselves.

Intimacy is also a practice. We have to make an effort. Many of us are geared more toward hiding than exposing our vulnerabilities, so intimacy requires deliberate intent. And like love, intimacy also has to start as an inside job. We can't receive love or intimacy from someone else until we give it to ourselves. In other words, the amount of intimacy you're able to have in a relationship is directly proportionate to how intimate you are with yourself.

During my marriage, I wasn't much more intimate with myself than I was with my husband. I didn't want to see my own foibles or own up to the fact that I wasn't happy in the relationship. I was too busy trying to live up to the image I'd created and keep up the pretense that my husband and I were the perfect couple.

I wanted intimacy deeply, yet I wasn't making myself available for it. It just goes to show that we can want something we're not actually available for, and we can be available for exactly what we don't want.

So this step is about redefining intimacy—no longer thinking of it in merely physical terms or as something we have to *get* from someone else. We need to be proactive within ourselves and in our relationships if we want an intimate connection.

Exercise #10: Meditation for Unconcealing Your Hiding Places

Intimacy involves letting ourselves be seen in the fullness of who we are. But first, we have to be willing to be the fullness of who we are. No mask and no false superhero cape allowed! But how do we do that? This meditation is a way you can begin to step into the fullness of you. You'll need time and space to be quiet for at least 20–30 minutes.

I know it can feel scary to explore the areas you've been hiding from yourself, so before you start, set an intention that you'll love yourself no matter what. Remind yourself that everyone has a so-called dark side, and everyone makes mistakes. You're a lovable person regardless, and every part of you deserves compassion and acceptance.

Meanwhile, ask the perfectionist part of you to go somewhere else. You'll do this meditation without that part of you, thank you very much. Then, take a deep breath and allow yourself to be here for yourself in this moment. Whatever you discover will be for your greater good.

Be sure to turn off all phones so that you can surrender to this process. Sit on a comfortable chair or couch in comfortable clothes. Feel free to play soft music or light candles, if you like. It helps to record your own voice reading the steps so that you don't have to open your eyes, which will disrupt your meditative state. Note that if you record it yourself, you may want to leave out the instructions in italics.

1. Close your eyes, and take several breaths. Relax each part of your body, starting with your feet. Then, gradually move up your legs, hips, belly, chest, back, arms, neck, and head until you feel fully relaxed. *Don't work too hard at this. Just ask your body to relax. As you continue, it will relax more and more.*

2. Now imagine that there's a door in front of you with a peephole at eye level. Behind the door is a secret, an emotion, or an aspect of you that you don't want to see.

3. Step up to the door, look through the peephole, and notice what you see. What's behind this door? Take a few moments to allow images or feelings to form, but don't force anything. The right information will arise naturally, and you can trust whatever you find. If you see nothing, release the blank space and ask your subconscious again for an image or feeling that relates to your deepest shame. You may repeat this if necessary until you get an impression. Don't worry if it takes a little while; you're excavating something from a very long time ago and it may be a little tender and/or shy.

79

4. Name the shame that has caused you to hide this image or feeling. Do you fear it makes you "bad" or "unlovable"?

5. What do you fear would happen if someone else knew about this?

6. How have you kept this aspect of yourself at bay? Do you distract yourself with another activity such as exercise, or do you fall into addictive behavior to avoid it, such as drinking, eating, or excessive shopping? Try to be as honest and open-minded with yourself as you can be.

7. What would it take for you to love yourself anyway?

8. Imagine the person who loves you most in the world. Imagine this person is with you now, telling you that you're still lovable. Allow this person to shower you with love. He or she might drop rose petals onto your body or envelop you in sparkling white light. Feel the love as best you can. Really take it in.

9. Now, if you can, open the door to the hiding place. As you do, extend that love to the part of you behind the door. Perhaps this part did something you've deemed unacceptable, or perhaps it seems to be something unacceptable. It might be an emotion you believe you shouldn't feel, a quality you believe you shouldn't have, or an act in your past that you feel ashamed of having done. Give this shamed part of you as much love, compassion, and acceptance as you can.

10. If you'd like, you can repeat steps 2–9, imagining another door appearing with

another peephole, behind which something else you've hidden lies waiting.

11. When you're ready, open your eyes and write down what you remember from your inner exploration.

How Emotionally Intimate Should You Be While Dating?

We put our best foot forward when we date, expending a great deal of energy trying to manage how others perceive us. When we let that go, there's so much more energy available to us. Being on our "best behavior" is unsustainable, and the fall from the pedestal can be painful. I'm sure you know what that feels like.

When we don't reveal ourselves to our partner or a potential partner, it's because we fear judgment. While that's a valid fear to some degree, the judgment already exists inside us as self-judgment. We wouldn't hide it if we didn't already think it was unacceptable and might elicit the criticism of others.

When we lean into self-love, we're authentic from the beginning of a relationship. That doesn't mean we dump all of our dirty laundry on the first date, but we don't put forth a false persona either.

During my first date with Aaron, I unleashed a three-hour monologue on him that disclosed everything about my life. Talk about a turnaround from the woman I used to be! I told him about my marriage, my affair, my divorce—the whole enchilada. The poor guy didn't know what hit him. (Actually, he told me later that he was so fixated on wanting to kiss me that he didn't hear a word I said. Maybe that was a good thing!)

But what I learned from that experience is that intimacy requires both discernment and calibration. You have to decide what and how much you disclose, as well as when you disclose it.

I suggest gradually disclosing more and more, and as soon as the relationship begins to become serious, revealing the most important parts of who you are and the life you lead. Whenever you aren't sure whether to disclose a certain piece of information, ask yourself: "What's the most self-honoring choice I could make right now?"

The key is to know in your heart that you're lovable, and if someone else doesn't see it, you're better off saying good-bye. I know that can be a tall order, but the more you lean into love, the more you'll be certain of what you deserve!

BRING VULNERABILITY INTO YOUR RELATIONSHIP

Now that you've begun to reveal more of yourself *to* yourself, the next step is to lift the veil to reveal yourself to your partner. If you aren't in a romantic relationship at the moment, you can practice this with close friends or family members so that you'll be ready when your next relationship begins.

How much and what specifically do you disclose? How do you jump into expressing vulnerability if you haven't done much (or any) of that in your relationship before? The prospect can be daunting, for sure. You may be tempted to just let the dam break and do a mind dump, revealing everything you've been holding back for years, like I did with Aaron. But as I said, it's up to you to discern what to disclose and when.

One of my clients has been dealing with this very issue. She's had an affair and wants to leave her marriage. She knows she has to sit down with her husband and tell him that she wants to separate, but should she also tell him about her affair? Will it be beneficial for him to know about it, considering it will be a double whammy for him? Only she can answer that question, because it depends on so many factors specific to the two of them. But the key is that we have to think before we speak.

When we want to open up to our partner, the most important questions to ask are: "What's my intention for disclosing this? What do I hope will happen if I reveal this? Telling this to my partner will be in service of *what*, specifically?" If it doesn't serve a positive purpose, it may be better left unsaid. There's no good reason, for example, to say something negative about your partner just to be truthful, especially if it's something he or she can't change.

It could be that your only reason for revealing something is to establish more closeness with him/her. You want to open up, be vulnerable, and get to know each other better. That's a perfectly valid and wonderful intention! But again, what do you disclose and how much? I recommend dipping your toe in the expression of your vulnerability and truth. Look for small reinforcements instead of massive changes. Learning to be more emotionally intimate with one another will, once again, be a progressive practice.

Try inviting your partner to sit down with you so that you can each tell the other something you've been shy about revealing. If the idea causes either of you to shake in your shoes, start with something that brings up mild feelings of vulnerability. It can be helpful to agree that you'll reveal something that is "neutral to positive," emotionally speaking, for starters. That way you can get some vulnerability practice without risking doing harm or getting hurt. This isn't a time to deal with grievances or conflicts!

If it feels comfortable to do so, hold hands while you talk. When each person finishes, the other one can simply say, "Thank you for being vulnerable with me." Then, the other begins speaking.

Make a pact with each other that you'll speak one at a time without interruption, commentary, or cross-talk. Agree that you'll both listen intently. Decide to check your expectations at the door, and agree not to verbalize judgments of the other person. If it would help you feel safer, you can even draw up a short written contract that each of you will sign agreeing to the terms of your container.

Notice that I said it makes sense to hide your judgmental thoughts from your partner during this exercise. Again, intention is everything. If what you disclose is going to serve no purpose but to hurt the other person, keep it to yourself. But avoiding judgments entirely is probably impossible. Judgments will come up toward the other person and toward yourself. The inner critic doesn't go away, and it's hard not to project those judgments onto others.

What we can do in those moments is say to our inner critic, "There you are. I was expecting you, but I'm going to ignore you right now." Then we can recognize our judgments for what they are—criticisms fueled by insecurity. They're shadows that we've disowned within ourselves. If we use these strategies, we're more likely to prevent the judgment from hijacking us emotionally.

When you're finished with your disclosures, you might also want to take turns talking about how it felt to be vulnerable with each other. Remember to allow whatever feelings come up. If you feel emotionally triggered, try to recognize it as a trigger. Know that it's your "meaning-making machine" at work and may not have anything to do with the truth.

How do you begin to recognize your triggers? Well, as soon as you become emotionally upset, you've been triggered. (Once again, if you're being abused physically or emotionally, that's different. In that case, please get some professional help. In this context, I'm talking about issues that may arise between you and your partner that aren't related to abuse.) We get triggered because some part of us hasn't healed from a trauma or hurt in the past. The natural response, then, is to point a finger at the other person, but the ninja move in this situation is to experiment with withholding blame. Then look within and ask yourself, "Why does this upset me? Have I had a similar experience in the past? Do I judge the part of myself that acts this way, indicating a shadow is at play?" The only reason we feel triggered is that we still have some Velcro that the other person's behavior can attach to. Remember my earlier story about being triggered by laziness? Because being lazy felt so dangerous to me as a child, I become triggered by someone else's laziness. Someone else who doesn't have that "Velcro" might simply see the behavior as relaxed.

Most important, if either of you becomes upset, keep reminding yourself that you're working toward creating a relationship container that will allow you to express whatever you feel. Again, that takes some practice, so *breathe!*

Note: If your partner becomes abusive—shaming, blaming, or violent—in the face of your vulnerability, the issues you're facing in the relationship likely require professional help. So first and foremost, understand that your vulnerabilities aren't shameful, and you don't deserve to be treated that way. Then seek out a counselor, couples coach, or therapist to help the two of you navigate these turbulent waters.

Exercise #11: Tune In to Yourself

Sometimes, we're so emotionally shut down that we fail to notice that we're unhappy and need to communicate a problem to our partner. This free-form exercise will train you to become more aware of your inner life—whatever is going on inside of you. As a result, you'll begin to notice more of what you feel, so that you can express yourself authentically to your partner. It can help you note when you've felt misunderstood, unheard, or disrespected before it escalates into a larger issue.

While this exercise isn't a meditation per se, it does require 10–30 minutes of quiet time by yourself. Read through the entire exercise before you begin.

1. Wear comfortable clothes, sit in a comfortable chair, and close your eyes.

2. Tune in to your body, your mind, and your heart as best you can. Begin to notice your sensations, feelings, and thoughts. You don't have to write them down. Just note each one as it comes and goes.

3. Ask yourself: "What am I feeling right now?" You don't necessarily have to name the feeling, but notice it.

4. Ask the question repeatedly so that you become accustomed to tuning in with yourself regularly.

5. You might notice all sorts of things, from the trivial to the important, such as:

   "The back of my knee is itching."
   "I think what I'm feeling now is kind of like depression. I don't know what it's about."
   "I feel sad because I really didn't like the way John snapped at me the other day. It brought up memories of my mother yelling at me."

"I feel like I want to laugh, remembering what my daughter said the other day."
"My neck is stiff on the left side."

6. You may or may not decide to do anything with what you notice, but if you become aware of an issue that you need to bring up to your partner, the rest of this chapter will help you communicate it in a healthy and loving way.

DIVE INTO DEEPER PLACES

Let's say you discovered an issue during the previous exercise that you want to discuss with your partner, but you're sure it's going to be difficult. The first question to ask yourself is whether that's absolutely true. Open your mind and make space for an outcome other than the one you expect. Also, remember that you have no control over, or responsibility for, your partner's reactions, which are based on his/her own origin story, beliefs, and underlying commitments. All you can do is communicate lovingly and control your own reactions.

I know it can feel extremely vulnerable and scary to bring up a potentially contentious subject. Yet if you sweep it under the rug, you not only forgo the intimacy you want, but you also put your relationship at risk. Unresolved hurts don't go away. They fester and come up in covert ways like little digs at your partner or finding surreptitious ways to punish each other. Maybe it comes out when you complain about your husband's scratchy beard or when you refuse to help your wife with the housework. Or in the worst-case scenario, it comes out in a big blowout that seriously threatens the future of your relationship. Many of my clients refuse to hear the whispers of discontent and hurt until they become screams. When we ignore the truth, we betray ourselves as well as the relationship.

Here's another way to think about it: When we don't address the issues between us and allow them to "sit in the air," they become like pollution that we breathe every day. It might be temporarily difficult to clean up that pollution, but the long-term benefits far outweigh the short-term pain. And if both parties are willing to make an effort, we can often move into a new level of closeness.

That was the experience for my client Sophia. Her husband had an affair six months before they got married, but he waited until nine years later to tell her. Recently they talked about her unresolved feelings. "I shared my heart with my husband, and it was one of the most profound discussions we've ever had. Neither of us yelled or blamed. I'd been journaling, and he asked what I was doing. So I told him I was doing an exercise from Nancy's group coaching. This led to why I wanted to join the group and why I still love him, but also sometimes still hurt inside from the betrayal.

"I told him I'll always love him, but I've been holding a sword over my own head for a long, long time. I also brought up that I can't live with him making excuses about not doing counseling or inner work. That's not where I live anymore, but it's his call. And the talk that came out of this was, hands down, the most authentic we've had yet. He said he can't go back and change things but loves me so much that he'll do whatever it takes. No more hiding behind excuses. I felt deeply heard for the first time in a long, long time.

"I also gave him the space to be heard. It was hard, but I came at it from a place of respect. This is really exhilarating, beautiful, and deep stuff. I'm loving the new me."

Anna had a similar experience when she found the courage to broach a difficult subject with her husband. "For more than a year, I wanted to tell close family members that I had an affair. My husband already knew about it, but I hadn't told him about my longing to be transparent within our family. Not wanting to open an old wound, I hesitated bringing this up, but recently I did.

"Two things happened. One—we were able to recognize and name fears and beliefs that we both had around telling our family. Two—we were able to hold each other delicately through the process. This created space for the most open discussion we've ever had about my affair.

"By opening the door to discomfort, we were able to name our needs, look at our desire to move forward, and recognize how our past and current choices were impacting our trajectory. We saw how our new level of trust and vulnerability has created safety for giving voice to feelings and emotions—ones we previously tried to hide in an attempt not to hurt the other person."

What about you—are there any issues you've been avoiding discussing with your partner out of fear, or are there issues you avoided in past relationships? If so, the next section will give you some communication strategies to make these kinds of conversations go more smoothly.

What If Your Partner Isn't Willing to Talk through Issues?

In our society, we aren't taught to have honest conversations with each other. If your relationship hasn't been honest up to this point, your partner may not be willing to have a vulnerable conversation with you. If that's the case, you could attempt to gently convince him/her to read this book, or you could ask your partner to see a therapist or counselor with you.

But the fact remains that some people will continue be resistant. If that's the case, weigh the benefits you receive against the liability of less intimacy. If the relationship works for you anyway, this may be a concession you decide to make. Just make that decision consciously rather than from a place of fear. Whatever choice you make, you can and should continue to work on building your own self-love. Your own growth doesn't have to stop no matter what.

COZY UP TO CONFLICT

We're raised to think a harmonious relationship means zero conflict, but as I said earlier in the book, conflict is going to arise. We're human beings, and we're not always going to see things the same. But we tend to believe that telling our truth will automatically result in conflict, so we end up shutting down communication and losing our chance at both intimacy and growth. Then the issues between us fester, and we make them mean something that may have nothing to do with reality.

So many of my clients have stories that illustrate this point. Something bothers us, but we don't tell our partner about it because we're convinced he/she will be upset. When we finally bring it up, it isn't such a big deal after all. Or we make up a story in our head about what our partner's behavior means about the issue. So we hide our true feelings.

Women are especially socialized to avoid expressing any feelings that might lead to conflict. But plenty of men play this same avoidance game, particularly when the emotion involves vulnerability. We're told, "Don't rock the boat" and "Just suck it up." But if we can reframe conflict, seeing it as an opportunity to grow rather than a danger to avoid, we can begin to build that relationship container—a container that's strong enough to withstand our disagreements.

In a relationship based on the new relationship blueprint, we must be willing to risk conflict by revealing what bothers us—even when it's hard or scary. Even when we're *right* that it's going to rock the boat. To achieve intimacy and a relationship as a spiritual practice, *the boat simply needs to be rocked!*

I call it "cozying up to conflict." I know this is the last thing any of us wants to do. I spent my whole 18-year marriage turning myself inside out to avoid it! But as I've been willing to rock the boat more and more often in my current relationship, I feel like the process has taken sandpaper to me—in a good way that has smoothed out my rough edges. Yes, it has made me raw at times, but the smoothed edges have been healing and allowed Aaron and me to be more intimate and truthful with each other.

When we "rub up" against another human being in a vulnerable way, it's a kind of "exfoliation" that gets rid of the layers that keep us hidden and afraid.

I know, I know. It doesn't sound like fun. Sandpaper? A rocking boat? You may be shivering just thinking about it. Some of you may feel like my client Maria, who experienced abuse in her family when she was a kid. She has terrible memories of her father yelling at her mother, and she recalls being locked in the bathroom with her mom while her father beat on the door. Conflict doesn't feel safe to her, so it's taken a great deal of effort for her to "cozy up to it" in a healthy way.

"It's the newest and most unfathomable of concepts to me," she says, "but I'm willing to see conflict differently. I definitely formed the belief that all conflict could end in violence—and that it meant something and someone was wrong. I also learned that I needed to be on guard at all times—that what I saw couldn't be trusted. So I needed to control my environment by controlling my own emotions very carefully and strategically."

If you have a similar feeling about conflict, be gentle with yourself as you begin to alter your experience of it. Don't try to rush toward change. Baby steps are fine.

Like Maria, it has taken me some time to embrace conflict, but if I can do it, so can you. Just remember the saying, "When you're hysterical, it's historical." If you find that your emotions are running particularly high, you're likely reexperiencing emotions you've been keeping under wraps since childhood. In this case, you might need to wait until you can calm down—and locate the original source of the emotional upsurge—before you rock that boat. I've found that it helps to take a deep breath. As I inhale, I imagine that I'm breathing in love. As I exhale, I allow the energy of fear to leave my body on my breath. Sometimes I even visualize it as darkness flowing out of my body. I continue to breathe in and out until the fear dissipates and the darkness feels emptied. Then I'm more ready to initiate a rational discussion.

But what happens if you get emotionally triggered and regret what you say? Well, you could call a "do-over." You could say, "I realize that I was running some old patterning just now, and I'd like to take a moment so that I can respond from a different place."

I also have a trick for when I'm struggling to see Aaron's point of view. I ask for a time-out and say, "I'll be right back." Then I go to another part of the house and look out a window. This change of position gives me a different perspective and helps me to see what he sees.

If I can't physically change position, I can accomplish this perspective change in my mind. I visualize myself moving to another part of the house and looking out a different window. It helps me to have empathy for his viewpoint without needing to abandon my own point of view. I find that this simple exercise, even if it's done internally, helps me to see his opinion through new eyes. Then I can view both of our perspectives as valid.

My client Charles tried this and had the same positive result. He gets up and moves to a different chair. That simple maneuver has helped him see his wife's point of view more easily, changing the entire conversation. "I went from thinking that she was attacking me to realizing that I wasn't listening to what she was saying or seeing how she was feeling," he says.

The next time you find yourself in this situation, unable to see the other person's point of view, move to another vantage point. Maybe it will help you broaden your perspective. It might help to ease whatever conflict the two of you are experiencing.

THE ART OF COMMUNICATION

I have to give some credit to our therapist, Raven Wells, for the success Aaron and I have had in achieving deeper intimacy and communicating successfully. Certainly, if your relationship has been contentious, you might prefer to have your first vulnerable reveal in the presence of a couples' therapist, if your partner's willing. That can help take the edge off the fear.

Raven says that "clear communication is an art. Humanity is inherently messy, and clear communication (especially in the midst of difficult dynamics) takes conscious effort." He stresses the importance of "heart-full" intentions, as well as learning to both speak and listen skillfully. In my experience, all of this takes practice.

Some of my clients have discovered that they need to improve their communication skills when conflict comes up in their relationship. Emily has realized that she needs to be aware of the energy she brings into her communications with others. "If I don't feel worthy of being heard, I'll bring that energy to the situation," she says. In that case, she's much less likely to feel heard, no matter what the other person does or doesn't do.

Sophia has learned to make some adjustments in her communication as well. "In my marriage, I tend to over-share and really put myself out there. I want him so much to be able to connect with me. He just won't. It wasn't until doing this work that I learned it's in my delivery. I was coming off in a demanding way without realizing it. My husband has been telling me for years that he doesn't like it when I say 'I need you to do this' and 'I need you to do that.' I'd tell him he was just too defensive and was misconstruing my words. As a result, he built walls, and it was frustrating. Now I can see where my own issues with perfectionism and disowned parts of myself have been projected onto him. I ended up becoming the demanding parent that I had growing up!"

Sophia has also noticed that when she communicates with more vulnerability, she feels less judgmental. "I want to honor his needs and his right to be heard as much as I want him to honor my needs and desire to be heard," she says.

The need to be right is another common problem that gets in the way. It causes couples to revisit the same issues over and over without either resolution or understanding. They try to convince the other person that they're "right" ad nauseam, and until the other person "gets it," they don't feel safe.

I've struggled with this myself. I used to think opinions were black or white. It had to be my perspective or the other person's with no middle ground. Since I'd sublimated my own needs so often, I felt I had to compromise myself in order to feel empathy and see the other person's point of view.

I think the need to be right becomes an issue when we approach conflict as black or white. We believe that if we can't assert that we're right, it means we're *wrong*. But that isn't the case. What I've learned is that disagreement doesn't mean one of us is right and the other person is wrong. We just have different opinions, and both opinions deserve validation.

Both sides have probably distorted the situation a bit, and we need to acknowledge our own distortion, even if we don't yet know what it is. It's important to acknowledge that we all have emotional issues that cloud the truth and prevent us from seeing the situation clearly. In most cases, feeling definitively "right" is, in and of itself, a distortion of the truth.

Raven offers these valuable tips for communicating with your partner when the conversation might bring up some conflict. This process may be simple, but that doesn't mean it's easy! We're so unconsciously predisposed to seeing from our own perspective that we frequently do whatever we can to avoid hearing someone else's opinion. So if you and your partner enter into this conversation, you can count that alone as a success, regardless of whether the issue feels resolved at the end. Just stay aware that it could be difficult at first, so if your partner is willing, keep at it. Practice, practice, practice!

1. If a vulnerable conversation is entirely new to your relationship, prepare your partner ahead of time. Let him or her know what to expect in advance. (Perhaps even share this chapter with him/her.)

2. Ask your partner if you can have a conversation about something that's bothering you.

3. Don't push if your partner isn't in the right emotional space for the conversation. If either of you is tired, preoccupied, or upset, it's best to postpone your talk. Of course, if your partner tries to put it off indefinitely, you'll have to gently push back and ask to schedule an opportune time.

4. Agree on an intention for your conversation that's heart-centered, such as "hearing each other with compassion and love" or "clearing the air with acceptance for whatever we're each feeling." Take a moment to connect with your hearts before you begin speaking. Commit yourselves to rising above your triggers and reactivity.

5. Studies show that expectations can have a tremendous impact on the outcome of our exchanges. Ask yourself if you have any expectations that could be negative, and replace them with more empowering ones. Here are Raven's examples:

   - "He's definitely too defensive to hear what I have to say" can be changed to "I trust him to hear me and be able to take in the feedback."

   - "I'll never be able to say this right. It's just going to make things worse" can be changed to "I'm totally capable of articulating this in a way that's not only clear but will create more of a connection between us."

- "She always turns everything around and makes it about her. It isn't even worth trying to talk about my side of things" can be changed to "She cares about what I have to say, and I expect to come out of this feeling like she listened to me well."

6. Start the conversation with positive, loving feedback for each other to set the tone. Take turns saying one thing you genuinely appreciate about each other.

7. In your conversation, focus on just one issue, even if you have several issues you want to address. Then, communicate just the simple facts, and discuss only the behavior that has had an effect on you.

8. Avoid accusatory, victim words like "you made me feel awful." Similarly, avoid absolutes and hyperboles like "you never treat me with respect" and "you always ignore my feelings."

9. Avoid trying to be right, and guard against raising your voice.

10. Don't rush the conversation. Speed is the enemy of connection.

11. If you're unable to reach an agreement, take a deep breath and affirm your love for one another despite the fact that you disagree. Remind yourself that you're safe even when the two of you don't have the same point of view.

12. End the conversation by sharing specific appreciation for each other again.

Exercise #12: Guidelines for Communicating Issues

The following is Raven's "Clear Communication" structure. Use this format whenever you need to discuss a potentially difficult issue with your partner.

Remember: Whenever you have a vulnerable conversation with your partner, bring with you all the love you have in your heart. Recall why you chose this person. Maybe even imagine your partner as a little boy or girl who was hurt and developed limiting beliefs, just like you. The more you can empathize with each other, the less likely the conversation will escalate into an argument. Then you'll be well on your way to true intimacy and a strong relationship container that will hold you both wherever you are in each moment.

Step One: The Speaker offers the most concise and accurate version they can: "When you did/said _____, the impact on me was _____."

The following is a menu of possible areas of impact:

1. *Story:* "The story I went into about it was _____."
   For example, what did you make the situation mean in your mind?

2. *Feelings:* "I felt angry" or "I felt happy" or "I felt sad" or "I felt betrayed."

3. *Body Experience:* "When you raised your voice, my stomach tightened, and it was hard

to breathe" or "When you cleaned the snow off my car, my shoulders relaxed."

4. *The Connection:* "I feel less trusting" or "I feel more open" or "I feel shut down to you."

Step Two, Part A: Using the Speaker's exact words, the Listener reflects back what he/she heard: "What I heard you say was _____. Is that complete and accurate?" Allow time for refinement if the Speaker needs to note what was missing in the reflection or add a point (keeping it short and to the essence of the discussion).

Step Two, Part B: The Listener validates the Speaker's experience through empathy and acknowledgment. This is done by articulating the story from the Speaker's perspective and finding language that conveys the Listener's understanding of the Speaker's experience. It's important for the Listener to show that he/she considers the Speaker's experience valid and cares about it emotionally: "If _____ had just happened to me, I'd feel _____, too." Or: "I can see why you felt that way because _____." Or: "It makes sense why you'd have that experience, since _____."

Step Three: Pause and see what's needed to feel complete. Remember that speed is the enemy of connection.

The turn is finished when the Speaker feels some sense of feeling heard. If all went well, at this point, there will be a greater openness between the Speaker and Listener. Take a moment to let that soak in. Allow for a little spaciousness, and an organic next step might arise.

This is a good time for any of the following:

- The Listener naming how he/she feels about his/her impact on the Speaker: "I'm honored to know you feel that way" or "It pains me to know how much my actions upset you."

- Making commitments: "I'll do my best in the future to call when I know I'm going to be late."

- Stating preferences and needs: "I'd prefer you ask me first before agreeing to plans that involve me" or "I have a need to feel respected" or "I'd prefer it if you spoke more slowly."

Once the cycle has completed for one Speaker and Listener, you may want to reverse roles so that the other person can take a turn as the Speaker. You might also need to go through another cycle in order to fully clear the air on the subject.

Relationship Reframe

"I continuously cultivate greater levels of intimacy with myself and my partner, allowing all of me to be seen."

Step 6

Embrace Selfishness

I believe selfishness is the foundation of a great relationship. There, I said it.

I know, I know—it's controversial. Just the thought triggers a lot of people.

When I suggested to a caller on my Hay House Radio show that she make herself a priority, she exclaimed in horror, "Isn't that *selfish*?!?!"

"Yes," I said. "Exactly!"

Someone else commented, "Selfishness is just an excuse to treat others badly."

So let me be clear: That isn't the kind of selfishness I'm talking about. We've already redefined intimacy; now, it's time to redefine selfishness. I'm not advocating that you walk all over someone else's feelings and take care of your own needs without ever taking your partner into consideration. The new, more "selfish" version of you will still care deeply, and you'll even make compromises now and then. You'll genuinely want to do things for others, but it won't come from a "people-pleasing" place, which is motivated by the need to prove your worth.

What I'm suggesting is simply to start holding your own needs as *equally important* to your partner's.

I've found that this concept is literally inconceivable to many of my clients. So few of us know how to honor our own needs when there are other people in the picture.

It may seem easier to prioritize your own needs when you're single. But from what I've observed, those who let go of their own needs when they're in relationship are usually not taking super good care of themselves even when they're alone. That said, working on good self-care when out of a relationship can be considered practice for partnership. Once you know how to love and care for yourself, it becomes harder and harder to abandon yourself when you're with someone else.

Stop right now and ask yourself this question, either about your current relationship or past relationships: Of these three, what order of importance do you give them?

- me
- my partner
- the relationship

Think about it carefully. Who or what is number one? Where do you fit in? For most of my clients, the order goes like this:

1. my partner
2. the relationship
3. me

And that's if they consider their own wants and needs at all—which not all of them do. More than once, I've asked a client what she wants with regard to her relationship, and she'll answer, "Well, *he* thinks we should . . ." Her own desires aren't even a part of the equation. While this is particularly common in women, some of my male clients fall into the same trap.

As you know, I'm personally familiar with this habit. For years I sublimated my own needs to try to keep my husband's love. My intense self-denial is no doubt one of the reasons I ended up having an affair. That's why I learned an important lesson in my marriage: Martyrdom, self-sacrifice, and people-pleasing lead to resentment, which creates discord in our relationships. When we consistently repress our own wants in deference to others, making sure everyone else but us is pleased, our true feelings are guaranteed to come out sideways. Resentments pile up, and we snap. Those resentments also rob us of so much energy that we could use toward loving ourselves and others. As my client Emily puts it, "Sacrifice is not a gift to the people we love."

For many of us, the self-denial goes on for decades. Eventually and inevitably, it comes back to haunt us. We may become ill, mentally or physically. Or something else dire happens to force us to change, as in my case when my husband read my journals and discovered my affair.

But these difficulties are not the only option we have. We can also learn to change the pattern *before* there's a blowup. The change we must make is to develop a healthy selfishness—the kind where we attend to our inner and outer needs.

The only relationship hierarchy that works in the long run is one in which you are *your number-one priority.* If, as I said earlier in the book, the new relationship blueprint means we're no longer shouldering the burden of our partner's needs or counting on them to take care of ours, why *shouldn't* we be number one on the list? Yes, we negotiate with each other, but we don't defer about what's truly important to us—*even if our partner doesn't like it.* And vice versa: We also have to be willing to let our partner put their own needs first and not expect them to take care of ours.

I now assume that what's best for me is what's best for my relationship. If I do what *isn't* best for me, the relationship will suffer—because *I* am suffering. And the same goes for Aaron. In fact, I've found that when we're aligned with our own best interests, everything else seems to sort itself out.

It goes without saying that I'm talking about reasonable needs and desires, not license to empty your joint bank account on a gambling trip to Vegas. There's a balance to be achieved here. The problem is that for most of us, the scale has too long been tipped toward everyone but ourselves.

That's what I want to remedy in this step, which is about embracing healthy selfishness and taking responsibility for our own choices. What would it feel like to care about yourself *at least* as much as you care about your partner?

What If You Have Kids?

I'm sure some of you are thinking, "Nancy, this is all fine and good if you don't have children. But when kids are involved, your own needs just don't matter anymore." It's true that my ex and I didn't have kids, but if we had, I'm sure I would have put their needs above my own 100 percent. And my clients with children usually end up as number four on the priority list: kids first, then partner, then the relationship, and then themselves.

Certainly, if you have kids who are still of dependent age, they'll be number one most of the time. That's the way it's supposed to be. But even with young children, you can—and really, you *must*—find opportunities to take care of you.

Have you ever gotten angry at your kids because you felt resentful of all they need from you? Because you denied yourself for so long that you snapped? If you give yourself an opportunity to fulfill your own needs when it's feasible, the snapping will happen less often. Plus, taking care of yourself models self-care for your kids, teaching them what it looks like to love themselves.

If your kids aren't accustomed to you taking time for yourself, you might have to sit down and have a candid talk with them about why it's important. My client Valerie is having some problems with her 20-year-old daughter, who thinks it's "rude" for her mom to make plans on her own. If Valerie sits down with her daughter and explains what she's learned from this book and our coaching together, I'm hopeful that it will be a teaching moment to help her daughter become less dependent. And it will allow Valerie to have the time and space she needs for her own self-nourishment.

"STAYING HOME" WITHIN YOURSELF

Before you can ask for what you want, you have to figure out what that is! To do that, you must "stay home" within yourself like you did in Exercise #11 in Step 5. The result? (1) You become aware of your own wants, and (2) you start allowing those wants to be just as important as anyone else's.

In Exercise #11, you began to check in with yourself to notice more of your feelings and body sensations. Another way to stay home is by taking a moment to deliberately focus on yourself at the start of each day. I call this "anchoring into yourself." You can do it in bed before you get up and again whenever you feel the need throughout the day.

In the past, my first thought each morning was *What do I need to worry about today?* I've made a concerted effort to change that habit. Now I wake up and ask myself, *What's the most self-loving action I can take today? What's the most self-honoring choice I can make today?* This way, I'm anchoring my first thoughts to *me*, and focusing them on my own needs and desires.

Many of us lose ourselves the minute we intuit that someone we love is having a need or desire of their own. We might start out anchored, but someone else's waves can easily throw us off course. My client Maria, for example, has struggled to stay anchored in her own feelings. She says she used to "take the temperature" of her partner, waiting to gauge his behavior so that she could decide how to act. She hid her own feelings because she didn't feel worthy enough to express them or have what she wanted.

I suggest that you affirm each morning that you'll stay anchored in *you*. Take your *own* emotional temperature before anyone else's. Ask yourself what *you're* feeling and what *you* want. You'll soon become more aware of yourself and better able to make yourself a priority.

Once you have an idea of how you've automatically acquiesced to your partner's needs in the past, and you're more aware of your own wants and needs, the practice begins of catching yourself in the act of deferring to others. If you're in a romantic relationship, you can note when you do this with your partner. If not, check yourself with friends, family members, and co-workers.

My friend Rita says a former girlfriend complained, "We always do what you want to do!" Rita was stunned. She'd always assumed her friend agreed to her suggestions because she wanted to do the same thing. She would've been fine if it took them longer to find a movie or concert they *both* wanted to attend. But her friend felt she had to always agree to what Rita wanted. Then she felt put upon, even though she never voiced her own desires to Rita.

So before you acquiesce, stop and ask yourself what *you* want. Are you truly okay with doing what the other person wants, or do you want to ask for something different? Then practice stating what you'd prefer. Maybe your habit is to immediately ask, "Where would you like to have dinner?" Instead, try saying, "I'd like to try that Chinese restaurant tonight." Now, if the other person hates Chinese food, this is a time when compromise would make sense. Contrary to popular opinion, taking your own needs into account doesn't automatically mean you become rigid and dismissive of others. The goal is to take note of your own preferences, and speak up so you get what you want at least 50 percent of the time.

If the topic is more important than choosing a movie or a restaurant, you might initiate the conversation by saying, "I notice what I want here is _____, and I'm wondering what you want." This might feel more vulnerable, but it's honest, clear, and direct. It initiates a conversation in which you negotiate with each other and decide together what's best. While you may end up compromising at the end of that conversation, avoid doing it if you feel strongly that you need the opposite of what's proposed. Work toward putting yourself on equal footing with others.

If you've been acquiescing up until now, this new, more self-honoring way of being may need some time to take root. It might feel uncomfortably forceful at first to even name that you *have* needs and preferences. Some rigidity may even be necessary in order to overcome the expectation that you'll always defer. But once you're more comfortable stating what you want and making sure your needs are met, a balance will naturally be struck. It may be awkward in the beginning because you're developing a new skill. It was certainly clunky for me. But you'll get there!

Exercise #13: Learn to State What You Want

In this exercise, you'll recall times in romantic relationships when you've put your partner's needs and wants ahead of your own. This exploration will help you begin to notice when you acquiesce without thinking about your own desires first.

1. Think back to times in your current or last few relationships when you deferred to what your partner wanted. Let's say you and your partner were talking about seeing a movie or going to a restaurant. Did you wait for them to voice their opinion, and did you automatically agree? Did you acquiesce about more important aspects of the relationship such as not discussing a difficult issue because they didn't want to? Did you decide not to voice your objection to your partner's behavior out of the fear of conflict?

2. Make a list of the most important times you can remember when you didn't ask for what you wanted or times when you put your partner's needs before your own. What were the consequences of not speaking up? Did you miss out on getting what you wanted, and did you resent your partner for it? Did your partner miss out on getting to know you more fully? Having this list will help you watch for incidents in the future when you're on the verge of putting your own needs and

wants aside again. Watch for these moments in your life, and begin to gently coax yourself toward stating what you want.

FROM EITHER/OR TO BOTH/AND

Most of us relate to selfishness and selflessness as mutually exclusive. But they aren't. We live in a double bind, thinking *If I please myself, I disappoint you. If you please yourself, you disappoint me.* We believe that life is a zero-sum game—that if I have something, someone else goes without. Or if someone else has it, that means I go without. This is either/or thinking.

But life isn't a zero-sum game, and it isn't either/or. It's *both/and.* Self-care and self-love (healthy selfishness) don't have to come at the expense of other people.

The new relationship blueprint says that I can please myself, and that might disappoint you. But that's okay. You can please yourself, and it might disappoint me. And that's okay, too. Disappointment isn't fatal to the relationship unless we hold to the old blueprint belief that we're responsible for fulfilling each other's needs. The truth is that the relationship is much more at risk when we put our own choices and needs on the back burner.

In the old relationship blueprint, we feel we have to maintain harmony and reach consensus at any cost. But connection is more important than resolution or even harmony. When we maintain harmony at any cost our true self shuts down. Then it's easy to point the finger at the other person as the "cause of the problems" in the relationship. Often we feel anger toward our partner without knowing why. But when we *deny ourselves repeatedly*—maybe even for years—we're bound to feel angry.

So many of us have rejected selfishness to such a degree that we end up projecting it out onto others. It becomes one of our shadows. We find ourselves surrounded by people who exhibit what appears to us as selfish behavior, and we judge and blame them. But as we now know, when we're pointing fingers at other people, we need to look at ourselves. Because the qualities we find problematic in others are the very qualities we're failing to acknowledge inside of us. If we fail to integrate healthy selfishness within ourselves, we'll be offended by any whiff of self-care in others.

Redefining and embracing selfishness means we're willing to believe we're as worthy of receiving as our partner. It means we give to ourselves as much as (or more than) we give to others. It calls upon us to become comfortable with (1) identifying our own needs, (2) naming them to our partner, and (3) taking responsibility for seeing that they're met. It asks us to make our own self-nourishment a sacred necessity.

We can trust that both/and is possible. We can trust that our intimate relationships are capable of holding the truth of who we each are, as well as the differences between us. Then we can say, "Here's what I'm doing for myself in order to be me." Not asking for permission, but informing the other person gently and simply. We can be available to listen to and acknowledge their feelings about our decision, but the fact that they're having feelings doesn't require us to change our minds. Remember: To be true to ourselves and show up in our relationships authentically, the boat might have to be rocked!

Not long ago, I found myself in that old familiar double bind. Overwhelmed because I craved quality alone time, while Aaron wanted us to spend more time together. First, I tuned in to myself and recognized my desire for the alone time. Then, I let Aaron know that three mornings a week, I wouldn't be available for coffee together even though he cherishes that time with me. Instead, I'd be in my office by myself with the door closed.

It wasn't easy for me to tell him this, and it wasn't easy to do on that first day. I spent nearly the whole time writing in my journal about my discomfort with having set such a self-honoring and self-loving boundary. And Aaron wasn't happy about it either. But here's the deal: While I care about his comfort, my own comfort has to be my priority. The fact that he had feelings about it made me sad, but it wasn't worth abandoning myself for. He's a grown-up, and I can trust him to take care of himself.

By the second morning, I could already feel my "worthy muscle" beginning to strengthen. Even Aaron, who was reluctant at first, has started to relish that time to himself, which has been a lovely and unexpected by-product of my decision.

In our relationship, I've had to find a way to experience independence and freedom instead of the suffocation and drowning I felt in my marriage. I'm simply no longer willing to package myself in a way that makes me palatable to someone. Abandoning myself for the sake of another is no longer a badge of honor. In fact, it isn't even an option.

Now that I'm no longer trying to be seen in a certain light—and have stopped people-pleasing to buy love or even "like"—I find that it's okay to disappoint someone or rub them the wrong way. As long as I'm true to myself and express my needs with loving grace, I can easily move through any guilt or discomfort into the deep relief that comes with being fully myself.

This doesn't mean that I never extend myself for others—quite the contrary. For example, not long ago Aaron broke his collarbone during a mountain bike ride. He needed me to cook for him, bathe him, take him to surgery, and more. Now between you and me, none of those tasks are in my comfort zone. My mothering instincts are, shall we say, *low*. But, of course, I took care of him. Healthy selfishness leaves plenty of room for showing up when needed. In fact, it turned out to be a sweet few weeks of togetherness. Both/and means that we weigh each situation and make decisions based on self-love *and* our love for the other person. We don't make our decisions based on obligation or fear.

It's one thing to step up in a crisis, but it's another to believe that a "good woman" or "good man" is always going to be unselfish. That's a cultural belief we need to let go the way of the dinosaur. It's like when you're on an airplane. They tell you to put on your own oxygen mask first before you help anyone else, including a child. That's because you could pass out before you'd be able to help others. Many of us go almost that far—practically killing ourselves in service of other people, hoping somehow they will meet our needs in return. We empty our own pitcher to such a degree that we completely run out of juice. What can you pour out of a dry, empty pitcher? If we fill our own pitcher with self-love and self-care, we can live in a state of abundance—where we have love and care to shower on others.

My client Charles found this to be true when he began to take care of his own needs more often. "I'm not always prioritizing myself, but I'm taking myself into account in the decisions I make," he says. "And because I'm doing that, I'm able to do far more for my wife and others than I ever could have before. I think that's because I've lost the resentment."

He has also begun to negotiate with his wife. To his surprise, both of their needs often get met in the process. "She came to me last night for help," he told me recently, "saying, 'I've got these critical things to do for my business, which I need tomorrow.' I said, 'Look, I had planned on doing X, Y, and Z for *my* business. If you can help me get that done, then we can work on your stuff.' Her immediate reaction was 'Absolutely! Let's get it done.' In the past, I'd have said, 'Let's do what you need to get done,' and I'd have been quietly bitter that my own stuff didn't get done."

We have this belief that the "we" becomes diluted when we take "you time" and "me time." But I contend that the "we" gets stronger when we each take our "me time." That's how we truly receive the *both/and* benefits of being in a relationship.

TAKE RESPONSIBILITY FOR YOURSELF, NOT YOUR PARTNER

When we take responsibility for ourselves, as I've said, we know it's our own business to make sure our needs are met. We no longer expect our partner to do it for us. We also understand that we aren't responsible for our partner's feelings, and it's their job to take care of their own needs. Therefore, instead of saying to our partner, "I need *you* to do this," we recognize our own need and invite our partner to support us in it or not.

My client Peter says, "I'm more the needy one. If I don't allow myself to fill my own needs, I end up standing behind this wall that my wife's put up." When he makes the effort to understand her needs as different from his own, he can also see that her need for alone time doesn't mean she doesn't love him. And he doesn't require her to fill him anymore. In the past, there was often resentment on both sides. She felt put upon by his needs, and he felt rejected. Now each of them can take responsibility for themselves and come together when it's right for both of them, enjoying a deeper connection without the dissonance that was present before.

My client Rhonda puts it this way: "Under the old blueprint, I expected my partner to 'step up' and meet me where I am. Under the new blueprint, I 'step into' who I am, what I need, and what I want in order to bring a fuller version of me to the relationship negotiation table."

When we *don't* take responsibility for ourselves, we give up power and control, and we deny ourselves the ability to make positive changes. We become resigned to our lot in life and give up our hopes and dreams. In relationships, we relinquish our own needs, feeling that it's our job to take care of the other person no matter what and vice versa. Then we blame the other person when our own needs aren't met.

But taking responsibility means that we can no longer blame our partner if our needs don't get met. We have to let go of being a victim and embrace the truth that *we* create the circumstances in our lives. Nobody consciously creates unpleasant circumstances, but all of our beliefs, decisions, and actions over the years are choice points that have brought us to where we are right now. Every decision we make and every action we take contributes to the overall landscape of our lives and the events that happen within it.

When we take responsibility, we're empowered to make decisions and take actions that move us forward as individuals and as couples. It means we allow each relationship to be a spiritual practice that gives us countless opportunities to grow. We mine our experiences for insights, lessons, and information that will support us in moving toward what we want out of life. And even if we end up with disharmony and disappointment in our relationship, we give ourselves the opportunity to be truly loved for who we are—rather than for the façade we've created. When we show up authentically, we can create that container I keep talking about.

The container is actually a figurative space in which the two of you hold your mutual agreement to protect the relationship, ensuring it survives whatever disappointment or conflict comes up. You can even think of it as a resiliency that the two of you build up so that the connection and intimacy between you can withstand differences of opinion and emotional upheavals.

Within this container, we take responsibility for our own emotions rather than point the finger of blame toward our partner. We own and accept that we're the only person who can make any real changes in our life. We no longer wait for someone else to fix what isn't working, and we give up any desire to be rescued. No more fairy tales! No more princes scaling towers, and no kisses to wake us up.

Exercise #14: Meditation to Say Good-Bye to the Victim Within

In this meditation, you'll explore what it means to take the victim perspective, and what it means to do the opposite: to take responsibility for what happens in your life.

Set aside 20–30 minutes. Be sure to turn off all phones so that you can surrender to this process. Sit on a comfortable chair or couch in comfortable clothes. Feel free to play soft music or light candles, if you like. It helps to record your own voice reading the steps so that you don't have to open your eyes, which will disrupt your meditative state. You may wish to skip over recording the italicized portions within the meditation.

1. Close your eyes, and take several breaths. Relax each part of your body, starting with your feet. Then, gradually move up your legs, hips, belly, chest, back, arms, neck, and head until you feel fully relaxed. *Don't work too hard at this. Just ask your body to relax. As you continue, it will relax more and more.*

2. Take a deep breath, and allow a situation to come into your mind in which you played the role of the victim in a relationship, placing blame on your partner. Perhaps you put your own needs aside, overstepping your own boundaries, and then blamed your partner for it. What were you feeling? How did you put your own needs and desires aside? What motivated your behavior? Did you feel it was the only way to keep your partner? Were you afraid of being a "selfish" person? Tune in to the feelings, beliefs, thoughts, and internal dialogue that have kept you stuck in that place of victim. (Note that for this meditation, I'm not talking about a situation in which you were a victim of verbal or physical abuse.)

3. Take another deep breath, and acknowledge that standing in 100 percent responsibility means you co-created your current reality with the other participants in each circumstance. You did this to learn valuable lessons. Now consciously step out of the role of victim and step into the role of co-creator. From this vantage point, let yourself see where your responsibility lies in the situation

in which you played the victim. What choices did you make that led to where you are right now? What actions did you take that contributed to your current circumstances? What thoughts or beliefs did you hold on to that kept you from claiming your needs and taking responsibility for yourself?

4. As you breathe and digest all of this, let yourself identify a specific action or practice you can put in place this week to take more responsibility for your own needs. Is there something you want that you haven't mentioned to your partner yet? If you aren't currently in a relationship, is there something you aren't allowing yourself to have? Are you judging yourself for your selfishness or deferring your desires to others in your life? Where can you begin to let automatic acquiescence go and proclaim what you need?

5. Take a few moments to view your life and relationships through the new lens of responsibility. What looks different? How does it feel?

6. Make a commitment to take responsibility for yourself. Allow for any feelings to come up about this. You might feel a sense of freedom, or you may feel afraid of stepping into this new role. Or you might feel both! Just notice your feelings and know that taking responsibility and not falling back into the victim role will get easier with practice and time.

7. When you're ready, open your eyes and write down what you remember from your inner exploration.

IT'S YOUR CHOICE

We tend to assume that our desires will be in opposition to the good of others or that the desires of others will be in opposition to our own good. So we think we don't have choices in our relationships.

When we take responsibility for ourselves and recognize that a certain brand of selfishness can be healthy, we give ourselves freedom of choice. And this freedom gives us the ability to change our lives and our relationships for the better at any moment.

When we believe our choices are limited, however, we get into trouble. That's what happened to my client Emily. When she's doing artwork, she says, she doesn't like to be interrupted. "My husband, although perhaps well-meaning, likes to take care of me by making us both lunch. If he weren't here, I'd eat when I felt like coming up for air. But he puts lunch on the table, and like an obedient child, I rip myself out of creative mode and join him resentfully. Usually, I'll say that I want to get back to the piece I'm working on right after lunch.

"The other day, he said there was something he wanted to do after lunch, so he asked if I could help him with the dishes. I told him I'd do them on my own so that he could get back to his project. It was the least I could do to show my appreciation for the lunch I didn't want to eat, right? But he graciously declined my offer, saying he'd rather be a team doing the dishes. I felt irritated with him and his lunch. At the same time, I felt guilty for painting and not having more appreciation for his efforts. This has been a recurring theme."

Finally, Emily told her husband the truth about what she'd prefer. "When I'm in creative mode, I like to eat when it feels natural," she told him. "I don't want to be made to sit at the table and feel guilty for leaving the dishes. If you weren't here, I'd eat and wash the dishes after I finished painting."

It turned out that her husband didn't necessarily want to eat lunch at that time either. He simply felt he was supposed to take care of her and even felt some resentment about that "obligation" he had imposed on himself. Once they told each other the truth, they were both able to make the choices they truly wanted and let go of resentments that were needlessly poisoning their relationship.

"I used to believe that thinking or feeling differently was somehow mean or disrespectful," Emily says. "I'm learning that honesty is the most loving and authentic action I can take in our relationship."

Emily and her husband have agreed that they want to be truthful with one another, and now they ask for what they need without taking the other person's desires as a personal affront.

"Already, I can see that the choices my husband makes to do his own thing without me are awesome!" Emily says. "It gives me the space to do what I want by myself. I'm not creating a victim story anymore about what his independence means about me. I now understand that it doesn't mean anything. I'm celebrating his taking care of himself, and he's celebrating me being honest and claiming what I want for myself."

The new relationship blueprint is about how you love yourself first and foremost. Then the question is how you want to be loved by the other person. As you answer that question, you'll begin to discover where your desires overlap with the desires of your partner. *The intersection is where you create a healthy relationship.*

When we come from this perspective, we evaluate every decision first through the lens of "self," then the lens of "other," and finally the lens of "us."

If we want our life or our relationships to be different, all we have to do is make different choices. Again, that's our responsibility! Each choice we make dictates whether we struggle in frustration or live an extraordinary life—whether the choice is large or small, easy or difficult.

As Debbie Ford taught me, there are no such things as choices that matter and choices that don't—they *all* matter. Every one of our choices and actions leaves an imprint on our internal world and creates what happens to us in the outer world. They dictate the partners we attract and the relationships we have.

In a later chapter, you'll work on your vision for your own new relationship blueprint to help you make choices that are in alignment with that vision. In my experience, when you love and take care of yourself, you'll make choices each day that will attract better partners or improve your current relationship. You'll be your true self with your partner, so you'll feel loved for who you are. *And* you'll get your needs met—because most of the time, you'll meet them yourself.

Exercise #15: Your Freedom of Choice Meditation

In this meditation, you'll explore some of your choices in the past and what new choices you could make to change how you relate to selfishness. Give yourself 20–30 minutes.

Be sure to turn off all phones so that you can surrender to this process. Sit on a comfortable chair or couch in comfortable clothes. Feel free to play soft music or light candles, if you like. It helps to record your own voice reading the steps so that you

don't have to open your eyes, which will disrupt your medita-
tive state. You may wish to skip past the italicized portion of
the meditation while recording.

1. Close your eyes, and take several breaths.
    Relax each part of your body, starting with
    your feet. Then, gradually move up your legs,
    hips, belly, chest, back, arms, neck, and head
    until you feel fully relaxed. *Don't work too*
    hard at this. Just ask your body to relax. As you
    continue, it will relax more and more.

2. Take a deep breath, and let some of your past
    choices and actions come to mind—choices
    and actions that were out of alignment with
    self-love and self-care. What choices have
    you made—even the seemingly small ones—
    that have kept you bound to people-pleasing?

3. Allow yourself to see other choices you can
    start to make this week to move you in the
    direction of healthy selfishness.

4. Next, ask yourself: "What's the most self-
    loving action I can take today? What's
    the most self-honoring choice I can make
    today?" Listen for the answers. Then, make
    a commitment to take that action. It might
    be to take a walk, buy yourself flowers, or
    have a luxurious bath. It might be a few
    hours on your own or an overnight at a
    nearby hotel. It could be a conversation or
    decision that needs your attention. Keep it to
    something doable that day, but your action
    that day might involve planning a wonderful
    experience in the future, such as a trip
    somewhere exotic.

5. Lastly, ask yourself: "What would I have to know or believe in order to take 100 percent responsibility for my life and my ability to choose?" Hear the answer as a power statement or mantra. Breathe that message into every cell of your being. Feel it filling you and becoming your reality. Then, open your eyes, write it down, and post it on your wall, if you like.

Relationship Reframe

"For the good of myself, my relationship, and my family, I embrace healthy selfishness and make sure to take care of my own needs."

Step 7

Go It Alone for a While

When I was married, I became obsessed with the book *The Marriage Sabbatical: The Journey That Brings You Home* by Cheryl Jarvis. At the time, I felt a strong need for a break from married life, so I relished every word of that book. It's filled with stories of women throughout history who have taken "time off" from their relationships. Including the author, there are 56 women profiled from all walks of life. Their sabbaticals took a variety of forms.

Of course, men need a break, too, but history has been kinder to men who take sabbaticals. Nevertheless, there are plenty of men who feel they couldn't possibly take alone time. The excuses pile up for all of us: The household would fall apart. Nobody in my family would understand. And on and on.

I was one of those people who "couldn't possibly." Even though my husband and I didn't have children, I couldn't imagine my ex being able to survive without me. No matter how much I needed a break or how much *The Marriage Sabbatical* caused me to long for it, I didn't feel worthy of time to myself. I didn't believe I had the right to it.

It's an especially difficult concept for my clients who have kids—even if the kids are older. Jocelyn says, "For over 20 years, I was Queen Bee Mom. If it was something that interfered with me picking up/taking care of my kids, I didn't do it. If it involved the kids, I was the one and only one to take care of it. I occasionally asked for help, but I was still the one to 'figure everything out.' During that time, I never traveled by myself unless it was for work, and I rarely spent money on things for myself. I remember reading Shakti Gawain's book *Living in the Light* 30 years ago and thinking, 'Sleep when you're tired? Eat when you're hungry? That isn't possible! Who can do that?'"

Even without kids, my client Leah had a similar pattern. "I wouldn't allow myself to just sit down or take a nap. Sitting idle wasn't an option. I always had to be 'productive.' If I wasn't busy, then I was lazy. I never allowed myself to enjoy doing the things I love because others thought they were 'frivolous' or a 'waste of time.' I would never allow myself to have fun because there were so many other things that needed my attention."

I can relate. I used to think fun was frivolous, and laziness remains my number-one trigger. It took a lot of work for me to get to the point where I could not only allow for a sabbatical, but welcome and cherish it.

I worked on myself for a while, including deep work on past traumas. As a result, it became clear that I need to be alone periodically to regroup, check in with my feelings, and think about what I want. I believe this is true for most people, but few are aware of this need. They don't entertain the thought because it's so foreign to the old relationship blueprint that says we have to stay enmeshed in the relationship at all times. That old model tells us something's wrong if we need alone time. Maybe it comes from the notion that we become "one" when we're coupled, but I believe that's a romantic idea that has little to do with reality. It's also been used as an excuse for steering clear of the discomfort required when we set healthy boundaries.

In the previous chapter, we talked about "me time." Going it alone for a while is the ultimate "me time." But for most of us, it takes a considerable amount of rewiring to believe we have the right to it. As we talked about in Step 6, we have to come to terms with the fact that our own needs matter, and that denying our needs does nothing to create a more harmonious relationship. It doesn't make us better parents either.

It can be difficult when your family expects you to always be available. They aren't accustomed to you taking care of yourself, and the change feels uncomfortable and potentially destabilizing. As a result, we defer back to our old ways. My client Valerie has this issue. She's tried to schedule time for herself, but she habitually allows her boundaries to be violated. "If someone wants or needs me, I'll often rearrange or forgo the time I set aside for myself," she says.

Often the objections are actually our own. Feeling like the world will stop turning without us is a way to maintain a sense of power and specialness. If we were to announce that we need some alone time, we'd find that our family doesn't object at all—or at least not nearly as much as we anticipated. That's what happened for my client Emily. "What surprised me the most is that my husband wasn't always honest about what he needs in the relationship either. We both sacrificed what we needed, thinking that's what the other person wanted. In fact, he wanted me to be fulfilled, and I wanted him to be fulfilled."

Luckily, there are ways to ease into your "go it alone time." You don't necessarily have to go away for a week, and you don't have to have money to accomplish this. We'll talk about the "how" later in the chapter.

Then there are those of you who are single and feel you're already alone too much. You might be thinking, *I thought this book was going to help me create a new relationship!* You may hate being alone or may not know what to do with yourself when you're "by yourself" or without a to-do list. Stay with me because I'm going to address all of that in the next few pages. I haven't forgotten about you!

Whether you're in a relationship right now or currently single, this step is about *taking a sabbatical from the ordinary in order to deepen your relationship with yourself.* Doing this will strengthen your relationships with others in the process.

Exercise #16: Flip the Script on Your Excuses

Before we move on, let's explore whatever fears you have about taking alone time and find out what excuses you use to avoid it. Then we'll flip the script and turn those excuses into positive affirmations.

Part 1—Pinpoint Your Fears

To unearth your feelings about alone time, write down your answers to these questions:

1. What am I afraid would happen if I took time for myself? What are my primary objections?

2. Have I judged others who have taken "me time"?

3. What do I fear my partner or family would say if I proposed taking time off?

4. If I feel like I'm isolating myself too

much already, what can I do to begin
to incorporate more social experiences
into my life?

Part 2—Explore Your Objections

What objections come up for you when you think about going it alone for an hour, a day, a weekend, or a week? Finish this sentence: "I can't take time alone because _____."

Keep completing the sentence until you have no more objections. My clients have finished their sentences with statements like "I don't have the money or the time" or "My husband/kids would freak out!" or "I don't want to take alone time because I'm already alone all the time as it is."

Part 3—Rewrite Your Script

Next, flip the script on your resistance. Take your sentences from Part 2, and rewrite them. Here are some examples:

Example #1: *Let's say your objection sentence is "I can't take time alone because I don't have the money or the time." Rewrite your sentence as: "I can and will take time alone because I'll make the time for myself, and I don't need money to do it."*

Example #2: *"I can't take time alone because my husband/kids will freak out!" Rewrite your sentence as: "I can and will take time alone because my husband and kids will understand once I explain to them that it will make me a better wife and mother. If they don't get it right away, they will in time."*

Example #3: *"I can't take alone time because I'm already alone all the time as it is." Rewrite your sentence as: "I can take alone time with the express purpose of nurturing myself more and learning how to love myself/fill my own needs better."*

Part 4—Make Your Plan

If you feel guilty about taking time for yourself, know that the guilty feelings aren't necessarily justified. It's common in the beginning to feel some guilt when you take alone time because you aren't accustomed to it. But eventually, the guilt will resolve. In the meantime, remind yourself of the costs of resentment. Remember that self-care is like money in the bank. When you use it up, you go bankrupt. Then you become stressed, which does no one around you any favors. You have to keep replenishing your self-care account in order to be your best self. With that in mind, make a plan to take some alone time this week.

WE ALL NEED A "PATTERN INTERRUPT"

"A break from dating? I've been on a forced sabbatical from relationship for 40 years," my client Elizabeth says. "I don't even remember the last time I went on a real date. I can't find a single soul to date, or they can't find me. Do you know how many trips, monthlong vacations, retreats, dinners, theater, and weddings I've done on my own? I've done countless real sabbaticals for months. So I've been a master at time with myself, and 40 years is a long time to enjoy that. I don't feel that anyone except women like me understand the challenge of being perpetually single and spending so much time on yourself. When people say, 'Oh, maybe you should enjoy time on your own,' I think, *Dude, when do I get to stop working on me?"*

I'm sure some of you reading this right now can relate to Elizabeth. I get it. If you've been on your own for a long time, the last thing you want to hear is that you need *more* alone time. But let me answer Elizabeth's last question, "When do I get to stop working on me?" You never stop working on yourself. A better question is: When does that work produce results? The answer is *when it does*, and it produces results with regard to relationships when both parties are consciously ready.

Whether you're single or in a relationship, the truth is the same: If what you want consciously differs from what you're getting, it means that there's an underlying commitment to staying alone. If your work thus far hasn't helped you discover and work on dismantling that underlying commitment, you have more work to do.

Here's another truth: If your behavior and mind-set stay the same, you'll get the same outcome. As the saying goes, "If you always do what you've always done, you'll always get what you've always got."

So even if you've been single and alone for an extended period of time, you need a "pattern interrupt" as much as someone who has been married for decades. You need to do something different.

I know that can be frustrating to hear, but remember what I said at the beginning of the book: My aim isn't to help you find a mate. It's about creating a healthier relationship with *yourself*. If you change the relationship blueprint in your mind, I believe you'll be much more open to a healthy relationship with a romantic partner, which might make you more likely to attract one. At the very least, you'll be prepared when he/she arrives.

My client Michelle says, "I resist being alone when what I want is to share my life with an intimate partner. I can't seem to get that fairy tale out of my head. Who doesn't want to be swept off their feet? I'm happy to do the work and try my new skills, and I like my independence and freedom. Yet I still wonder where he is."

If, like Michelle, you're feeling impatient or desperate about finding a relationship, I recommend that you go back to Steps 1 and 2. Do a deeper dive into your limiting beliefs and underlying commitments. Then connect with the parts of you that still believe a relationship is going to save you, and work with those parts to release that belief. If you need help, engage a therapist or coach if you can.

I asked both Elizabeth and Michelle if they could also begin to shift their single days from feelings of resentment and desperation to living more *intentionally*. While we're not working with the Law of Attraction in this book, one of the basic principles of that law is that we get more of what we focus on. So what happens when your focus is on what you *don't* have?

My guess is that if you're reading this book, you want to change your current circumstances with regard to relationships. Whatever those circumstances are, the pattern interrupt is essential. You need to regroup and change the way you think about relationships. If you're currently without an intimate partner, you can begin to put some of these principles into practice with the other people in your life. For example, you can begin to identify when you project your shadow selves onto friends, co-workers, or family members. You can strengthen your intimacy with yourself through working on the exercises in this book. Then you'll be able to create deeper intimacy with a partner when he/she comes into your life.

Remember: It's a habit to think nourishment is going to come from outside of us. A relationship will bring you many benefits, including a new mode of self-discovery, but as I've said before, it won't fill all of your needs. Very often, it doesn't even quell our feelings of loneliness, which were established when we were children.

When the next relationship comes, you'll probably find yourself pining for the time when you could make decisions without taking anyone else into account. So I suggest thinking about what you believe a relationship will provide for you, and look for ways to provide that for yourself. For example, if you believe a relationship will help you feel more secure, how can you give yourself a greater feeling of security? Which parts of you feel that lack of security? It might be as simple as talking with those parts of you and reminding them that you're just as secure on your own as with someone else.

If you believe a relationship will bring you love, give yourself more love. If you want a relationship for the closeness, try to be closer to your inner self. I'm not pretending that this is a substitute for another human being, but this act of giving yourself what you need might actually bring you exactly what you want.

Most important, honor the space between "no longer" and "not yet." This pattern interrupt is either a sabbatical from the relationship you're in—or the relationship you're *desperate* to be in. If you've been dating, that means taking a break from it, perhaps for a month. That's what Michelle has decided to do. "I intentionally got off all of the dating websites. It was seriously exhausting, so I just stopped," she says. "I put a date on the calendar to get back to it. My friends ask me all the time, 'Are you dating? Are you dating?' And lately, I've been saying, 'No, I'm not right now.'"

Michelle gets to choose the story she tells herself about it. She could choose "Woe is me" or "Look at the freedom I have" or "I'm learning about myself so that I can have a healthier relationship when the time is right." It doesn't mean her desire for a relationship goes away. But if she takes the time to center herself, she can loosen any feelings of desperation.

Elizabeth may need to reframe how she thinks about dating and her perceived lack of opportunities. She could change the story she tells herself and what she believes her life lacks without a partner. She could spend her time excavating the unconscious beliefs she carries about romantic relationship—both what it will offer her, and what may secretly feel dangerous about it. And she could begin to work toward providing herself with whatever she believes a relationship is going to offer her.

It's her inner child that feels disappointed. But our inner children can't see that if we think the only true sources of love are outside of us, love will only be an occasional visitor in our lives. If it comes from our own well, it's always ours.

The truth is that our inner children just want love and don't really care where that love comes from. So when we actually *do* love ourselves, we discover that there's no better feeling in the world.

Of course, the disappointment will likely come up again. But when it does, we can recognize it as the child's insatiable longing. We can accept the disappointment and sit with it rather than immediately label it as something "wrong" or something that we have to escape. Longing is a natural human emotion. We all feel it, and it may never go away entirely—not even within so-called "perfect" marriages.

Ask yourself: What's the longing about? Do I feel that I'm incomplete without a relationship? Do I feel like I "should" be coupled? Am I lonely? What can I do to ease the loneliness at least to some degree? Let's explore that in a meditation.

Exercise #17: Meditation on Patterns

In this meditation, you'll explore what patterns in your life might need to be interrupted. Give yourself 20–30 minutes.

Before we start, take a look at the patterns you wrote down on your Relationship Timeline. You might want to explore some of these, or new patterns might come to mind during the meditation.

Be sure to turn off all phones so that you can surrender to this process. Sit on a comfortable chair or couch in comfortable clothes. Feel free to play soft music or light candles, if you like. It helps to record your own voice reading the steps so that you don't have to open your eyes, which will disrupt your meditative state. You may wish to skip over the italicized portions of the meditation when you record.

1. Close your eyes, and take several breaths. Relax each part of your body, starting with your feet. Then, gradually move up your legs, hips, belly, chest, back, arms, neck, and head until you feel fully relaxed. *Don't work too hard at this. Just ask your body to relax. As you continue, it will relax more and more.*

2. Think about the person you most love in the world, someone where the love is uncomplicated and pure. Perhaps a child, a grandparent, or a friend. Feel your heart filling with that love. It might appear as a bright light. Now allow that love to fill your body from the top of your head to the tips of your toes. Allow yourself to take in this love that you feel for the other person.

3. Now turn this love toward yourself. Picture yourself as a young child, maybe as young as two, three, or four years old. See the little one you were, and give as much of this love to yourself as you can, knowing that you're still this young child deep within. Know that you deserve this love just as much as the other person you love so deeply.

4. Now that you've filled yourself with love, think about what dissatisfies you right now with regard to relationships. What isn't making you happy? Do you feel you don't have enough of a connection with your partner? Are you and your partner not getting along? Are you sick of being single? How long have you been dissatisfied?

5. Has this pattern played out in other relationships? Have you felt these same feelings for a previous partner, and maybe one before that? Or have you been single and alone for a long time? If you've been single for a while, that is a pattern in and of itself. But you may also want to reflect on the patterns you've experienced when you've been in previous intimate relationships. What patterns have recurred in your romantic life?

6. Now think about these questions, allowing time for the answers to come to you: What patterns in your life need to be resolved? Are there any recurring situations or feelings that you aren't aware of yet? What's the most critical pattern for you to work on right now?

7. What's the most important thing you can do to interrupt this pattern? What will heal this situation in your life?

8. When you're ready, open your eyes and write down what you heard so that you won't forget. During your first pattern interrupt sabbatical, reflect on what you learned about yourself in this meditation. Then, using the tools you've learned in this book, begin to work on dismantling the patterns that have kept you dissatisfied.

LEARNING TO LOVE YOUR OWN COMPANY

Some of my clients find that they relish their time alone when they're in a couple, but after they split up and become single again, they hate it.

Others dislike being alone no matter what. If they go to a movie or a restaurant without a companion, they feel like everybody notices and feels sorry for them. If they're home alone, they're so uncomfortable that they have to keep busy or turn on the TV to fill the empty space. If their partner is around, they have to always be with him/her.

All of these situations are indicators that we need to deepen our relationship with self, learn to love our own company, and strengthen our self-love. This requires compassion for our foibles and "failures." It involves recognizing our perfectionist voice and counteracting it with a loving voice that allows us to be human.

If you think of being alone as "by yourself," I encourage you to reframe it to being *"with* yourself." Even if you've been single and alone for a long time like Elizabeth, you can use the time while you're looking for a new relationship to become even more acquainted with yourself. In fact, such deeper self-knowledge may be exactly the thing your soul is wanting, and it may be the hidden reason you're not presently in a relationship. This is prime time to explore self-awareness practices. Try doing dream work, keeping a dream journal by your bedside, and learning about dream analysis to discover more about your innermost self. Or learn new ways to express your creativity, such as taking up a form of art—perhaps painting, writing, dancing, or ceramics.

If you aren't accustomed to spending time with yourself, your mini-sabbatical can be an opportunity to discover you're capable of more than you realized. My client

Leah had a chance to go to Paris for two weeks by herself, and since traveling alone was a new experience, it brought up a lot of fears for her. "What if I get lost? What about the money? Who's going to take care of my parents while I'm gone? What about terrorists? What if my luggage gets lost? I don't know the language! I don't know anybody there!"

But she went anyway. "One of the benefits," she says, "was no obligations. There was nothing I had to do. Only what I wanted to do. But it truly made me face my fears of uncertainty, embrace the unknown, let go of control, and rely on myself."

My friend Alice says, "I've spent a lot of my life uncoupled, and I don't let it stop me for a second. If I want to do something, I do it, whether it's a trip to Thailand or a seat at the theater or an event. I've learned to enjoy my own company and meet people wherever I go. One of my friends said she'd be embarrassed to show up at our high school reunion uncoupled or go to a wedding without a date. I feel like it's the other person's problem if they judge me for not having someone on my arm. All of this took some practice, but I've become increasingly extroverted as I've put myself out there and become more comfortable with social situations. I love spending time with others, but I also love being with myself, whether I'm just relaxing or in deep introspection."

Loving your own company is a skill you develop only by taking time with yourself and falling in love with who you are. If you struggle to enjoy your own company, I invite you to walk through the early discomfort of your time alone until you come out the other side, like my client Claire. "Four years ago when I lost my job, I had no idea how to be alone," she says. "I remember fidgeting and not even being comfortable enough to do something fun by myself. I really had to work at it. I started to evolve in my ability to be alone, and I came to love it so much that it would be foreign to me now to not take alone time. It's so important to me."

Your "Worst-Case Scenario Mantra"

If you feel you've already done all the personal work you can think of, it may be time to bring in the big guns. Bruce Tift, longtime Buddhist therapist and author of *Already Free*, has a powerful strategy for unearthing feelings we've held at bay for so many years that even the most powerful awareness practices don't touch them. He suggests writing yourself a worst-case scenario mantra—and coming to peace with it. If you are afraid you'll never find a partner, for example, your mantra might go like this: "I give myself permission to be single, alone, and lonely, on and off, for the rest of my life." Worst nightmare, right? But as they say, we only have power over that which we're willing to name. He encourages us to say our mantra out loud, several times a day. From his perspective we might as well acknowledge what already appears to be happening. While his approach may feel blunt, he's getting at a well-known truth—which is that what we resist persists. Rather than assuring his clients that they can have what they want and should just keep hoping, he sends them straight into the belly of the beast: having them speak, out loud, the possibility that things are never going to get any better. Then, he suggests letting whatever deep feelings arise be fully felt, such as grief, desolation, loneliness, and hopelessness. If we can become friends with them, even the "worst possible feelings in the world," a lot of frozen energy gets released. You'd be surprised what new opportunities start to arise once you've cleared the emotional space to make way for them.

PRACTICAL GUIDE TO A PERSONAL RETREAT

While I hope most of you will work your way up to taking at least one night away, if not a weekend, a week, or more, you can begin to give yourself alone time in small increments. For some of you, your obligations or finances might make it difficult to take even one night away. If this is truly the case, I am going to offer some shorter, free options in the pages that follow. But I have to mention that I often hear my clients using obligations and finances as an excuse. They can't take time for themselves, but they spend plenty of time each day watching TV and/or surfing Facebook. And they won't spend $89 on a night at a nearby Airbnb, but they'd spend that money in a heartbeat to indulge their children. Make sure you're not using these "very good arguments" as avoidance mechanisms!

I've heard several clients say some version of the following: "I can't take any time for myself until the dishes are done, the floors are vacuumed, and the bed is made." But what's more important—the cleanliness of your home, or *your happiness and enjoyment*? The floors will need to be vacuumed the next day, so letting them go one night (or even a few nights) isn't the end of the world. The same goes for leaving the dirty dishes in the sink.

Even if you don't have the money to spend an evening at a hotel or motel, you might have a friend who could loan you a house or apartment for a night when they're away. You might find that you've accumulated airline or credit card points that you can redeem for your night away. Check into it!

If you're a single mother with three toddlers, of course, I understand that time to yourself will be at a premium. But it can be done! And no, watching a TV show or ironing while your kids play in the same room doesn't count as alone time. Try trading child-sitting with another mother you trust, for example. She takes your kids while you get time with yourself, and you reciprocate later. If you don't know other mothers you can trust, seek them out!

Try getting a massage or a manicure if you can afford it. You'll at least have an hour devoted only to you. Or you could start by simply taking an hour for yourself one day a week after the kids go to school or after they go to sleep. Again, let the dishes sit! My hope is that you'll enjoy the time so much that you'll find ways to give yourself more, like an hour *five* days a week, leading up to a weekend away while the kids are with their grandparents and your spouse is getting his/her own "me time" at home.

I'm not trying to be preachy here, I simply want this me time *for you*, because it's when we're by ourselves that we can best hear our own needs, preferences, and desires. Are you willing to let go of the victim role that says you have no time and instead make yourself the priority? In my experience, when you open yourself up to possibility, the universe expands, and more possibility shows up.

Whatever challenges you have, if you're motivated enough, you can make it work. There's an author who wrote her book at 5 A.M. every morning while her kids were still asleep. Be creative and find ways to give yourself a small window of time.

As my client Jocelyn has said, "I wish my mother would have taken time for herself and shown me that model." If you have children, you'll set them up for that pattern in their own adulthood if you give yourself "me time" now.

For example, Anna's daughter is old enough that she's learning how to have quiet time even in the presence of her mom. "My daughter and I actually enjoy silence. We can be in each other's presence and not have to fill that space with words. I got stickers at the Omega Institute last summer that say 'In silence,' and when I brought them home, she said, 'Can I have some?' Even with homeschooling, we have a daily ritual where we both get alone time in the morning before we eat breakfast and start our day. So I'm much better at taking the time I need than I ever was. To integrate more alone time, I'm considering designating certain times each day as silent times when I don't have to interact and we do our separate things like read. I just have to get her set up with activities I know she likes, so I'm learning what resources I need to have on hand. What I've discovered is that whenever I give that gift of alone time to myself, I show up so much more present for everybody else when I reemerge."

While this isn't a sabbatical, per se, Charles and his spouse have found a way to be less enmeshed in their relationship even when they go to the same event. "When my wife and I go to conferences, we've actually matured to the point where she goes off in one direction while I go off in another direction," he says. "From the beginning of the day to the end of the day, we may see each other across the room, but we're now two individuals as opposed to 'Oh, that's Charles and his wife.'"

My client Tricia treats herself when she has a chance to be alone. "On Wednesdays and Thursdays, when I don't have my kids, I make myself a nice dinner," she says. "Financially, I'm not able to travel anywhere right now, and that's okay. But I really do try to find the time just to honor myself and be with myself."

Remember: If you take time for yourself, it doesn't mean you're taking away from the other people in your life. If you have kids, and you worry that they'll protest, try getting them involved. Explain to them in terms they can understand why it's important. Ask them to draw you a picture to take with you, paint a candle that you can burn during your time alone, or cut some flower petals for you to put in your bath water. Ask them what they think you should do while you're away. Make it a project that gives them an opportunity to show their love for you. This can work with teens as well.

My client Anna has discovered that her family understands more than she expected. "I've learned a lot about my family dynamic, and I see where we all get our needs met pretty easily if we just talk about what's alive for us in the moment and avoid stepping over our own needs in order to please another."

I also suggest looking for "me time" role models— people who do take time for themselves in a way that's palatable to you. As you do that, you might find people who take *too* much time for themselves in your opinion. If so, evaluate and question that judgment. Are they truly being *too* selfish? Maybe they are, but when you look at it from this new lens, maybe not.

If you don't have children or if they're grown, it will probably be easier for you to take your alone time, but you might have to convince your partner that it's important. Nevertheless, most of my clients have discovered that it's easier to get their partners on board than it is to talk themselves into taking the time. As we discussed in Step 6, you don't have to ask your partner for permission. You only have to give it to yourself.

For example, my client Claire and her boyfriend have worked out an arrangement so that she sleeps in the other bedroom by herself a few nights a week. "I love being able to watch TV until whatever time I want. I love being able to read with the light on. I love the puppy not jumping on the bed at 11:30 or 12:00 when I'm trying to fall asleep. We're only two feet away because my house isn't that big, but for me, it's been a game-changer that I'm allowed my sleep and comfort space," she says.

Sophia and her husband have begun to take trips separately when they want. Her first trip away on her own, she went to Hawaii for a conference. No one there knew her, and she loved the anonymity of it. "I didn't have to put masks on. I expressed this really fun part of myself. Some of my married friends couldn't believe I was leaving my husband by himself. But when I went back home, I was in a much better place. His needs were met, and mine were too," she says.

Whatever you plan to do for yourself, do it mindfully. Be as present with yourself as you can. Certainly, if you need downtime to binge-watch your favorite TV show, by all means do it. But be careful not to make that your habit. The idea is to get to know yourself better, to recharge, and to fill yourself with self-love. That requires purposeful nurturing, which might mean introspection and journaling. You may want to go to a meditation retreat or a spiritually oriented workshop if you can.

Be careful, too, when you return home. It takes a bit of time to sink back into the ordinary. One of the mistakes many of us make is trying to explain what we experienced to our loved ones. We want to share it with our partner or our family. Just bear in mind that it was *your* experience, and they may not be able to understand what it was like for you.

For most of us, taking alone time requires a commitment to ourselves. That's what Jocelyn had to do. "When we bought our house, I was adamant that I wanted a pretty front porch," she says. "I live in the South and have always had visions of sipping lemonade on the front porch on a hot summer afternoon and reading a book.

But I've lived in this house for over 10 years, and I'm not sure I've ever spent a lazy afternoon on my front porch. I'm committing this week to spending one hour on the porch reading a book that lights me up."

Once you become accustomed to your alone time, I suggest making it a lifestyle. As I've said, I take time for myself three mornings a week before Aaron and I come together. How can you integrate your new habit into your life so that you don't hit a wall of frustration and say, "I've got to get out of here right now before I explode!"?

My client Claire has done just that. She's learned to take great pleasure in the "reenergizing bliss" of alone time. "I don't need anyone's approval or validation, so that just helps me strengthen my own needs," she says. "I can do my laundry when I want, clean when I want, sleep for however long I want, and make myself fabulous meals when I want. I can take the time to take my photos or write. Heck, I can dance around the house in my lingerie if I want. It allows me to learn about myself in order to become the best version of me—for myself first and then for others. I'm an important appointment to be kept!"

Exercise #18: Your Personal Sabbatical Plan

Let's brainstorm how you can begin to give yourself a sabbatical/pattern interrupt, whether it's short or long.

1. Review your objections and rewritten sentences from Exercise #16. Do you now feel less resistant to the idea of taking alone time?

2. If you hate the idea of spending time alone, write down why. What is it about being alone that disturbs you?

3. Can you begin to imagine yourself enjoying your own company? Take a moment to do that. What would it feel like to actually relish your time alone—even if you feel you've had too much of it?

4. If you're tired of being alone a lot already, write down how you can begin to change the energy of your time with yourself. What would it take to engineer your alone time so that you can't imagine anything better than an evening to yourself?

5. Without stopping to think how you'd make it work, write down what you'd love to do on your own. Would you adore spending a month in Paris? Would you love to do a two-week meditation retreat in the mountains? What would feel amazing to you?

6. Now ask yourself what you feel you can conceivably do. Can you get a massage this week? Can you take an hour for yourself three mornings a week? Can you spend a night or a weekend in a hotel or bed & breakfast? Can you trade time off with another mom? Can you take that meditation retreat in the mountains?

7. If you need to discuss it with your family, make notes about how you'll explain it to them so that you'll feel more prepared and less nervous.

8. Once you decide what you want to do, write a contract/permission slip for yourself that will hold you to your commitment: "I give myself permission and commit to taking

an hour three mornings a week to be with myself. This is nonnegotiable, and I won't allow anything other than a life-and-death emergency to get in the way of this time to love and care for myself."

Relationship Reframe

"I allow myself a pattern interrupt and spend quality time with myself to recharge and get to know myself better."

Hone Your New Relationship Skills

In 2014, on my birthday, Aaron and I broke up. We left each other, though still very much in love, because we felt we wanted different things. He's eight years younger than I am and has never been married. I, on the other hand, had been through an enmeshed, codependent marriage. Where he was looking for a full-time partner and playmate—and wanted to spend the majority of his time with that person—I was happily entrenched in my career that had me on the road for long stretches at a time. I was either working or recovering most of the time. Love and play felt like just more items on my to-do list, but I believed I could juggle it all and give myself fully to both my career and the relationship. That "Superwoman" belief ultimately stretched our relationship to its breaking point.

When we parted, Aaron helped me load my car in Aspen for the drive back to my house in Boulder. He even packed a spare head for my electric toothbrush to make sure I wouldn't be without one. Remember that we parted in love.

We stayed apart for eight months. During that time, I self-published my book, *Jump . . . And Your Life Will*

Appear, got my deal from Hay House to republish it under their imprint, and traveled extensively for speaking engagements and visits with family and friends. I woke up when I wanted and went to bed when I wanted. I ate what I wanted and watched what appealed to me on TV. I often hiked several hours a day. I firmly established my coaching business, which allowed me to take the giant leap of leaving my day job with Hay House. I'll be honest: It felt like being alone was far easier than being in a couple.

Then . . . something started to change. I began to long for the fun and play I'd had with Aaron—the full-moon camping trips, mountain biking, and yummy sex that were the hallmarks of our relationship. I missed the very things I'd spent our relationship resisting. It wasn't about being lonely or wanting a boyfriend. I was happily single, yet I missed *Aaron*. I missed *us*.

I had honored his request not to communicate . . . until a day in October, eight months after we parted, when I decided to take a risk and follow my heart. Here's some of what I e-mailed to Aaron:

> "I want to relinquish
>
> the rigid stronghold
>
> that's keeping us apart
>
> and let you know
>
> I miss you in my life
>
> I love you always
>
> I am in love with you still."

Here's part of what he wrote back:

"Thank you for reaching out. I appreciate the risk you took in doing so. After writing and rewriting you for the past two hours, I don't know what to say. It feels good to hear from you. I am crying."

As fate would have it, Aaron was going to be in Boulder that weekend, so two days later, we met for a walk, sat on a rock in the middle of Boulder Creek, and talked for four hours. It was as if everything had changed, and nothing had changed. We've been together ever since.

How have we made it work? In service of "doing our relationship differently," we openly acknowledged the pain of the past. We faced our fears, allowed for expansion and possibility, and built on what was always good between us. We continue to strive to be both independent and entwined, each successful in whatever way that means for us as individuals. We're "all-in" in this loving relationship where we speak our truth, yet don't get threatened or lose ourselves in codependent dynamics.

I've shifted the belief that being in relationship and being successful in my career are mutually exclusive. I now understand that while life might indeed be easier when alone, it can be fulfilling in a completely different way when shared.

All of this has been a tall order for us, but we haven't done it without help. When we decided to get back together, the first thing we did was agree to work with a therapist from the start. We didn't want to wait until something "went wrong" or we were in the midst of a big argument. We wanted a collaborative approach with a third party as a witness. Mostly, we wanted to hone our relationship skills so that we could support each other in creating as healthy a relationship as we could.

So this step is about doing just that—honing your relationship skills. It's about learning to navigate the differences that inevitably arise when you share your life with another human being. Note that while you'll learn a great deal from reading this chapter, I strongly suggest you work with a couples' therapist, counselor, or coach if at all possible.

BECOME AWARE OF COMMON RELATIONSHIP DYNAMICS

I mentioned Bruce Tift previously; he says the following about his relationship: "I think it's accurate to say that I have experienced being disturbed in my marriage every day of the four decades we've been together. She assures me that it's been the same for her. There she is, just being herself, and I'll have a sudden surge of irritation, impatience, anger, or feeling. I usually find feelings of sadness and grief. Just by being herself, my wife is almost guaranteed to touch some sore spot. By her proximity, she pushes against my tender spots, my vulnerabilities. Of course, every day, I also have feelings of comfort, appreciation, and affection. But those aren't the feelings that most of us find difficult to deal with."

Wow. And he's a Buddhist! I have come to agree with him wholeheartedly. "Disturbance" is unavoidable, and it's our teacher. The sooner we become comfortable with the fact that disturbance is natural and expected in relationships, the sooner we can stop the people-pleasing, the bending over backward, and trying to "make" the other person happy. It's a losing battle—we can't *make* another person happy. That's an inside job that they have to do for themselves.

Disturbance is different from cozying up to conflict, however, as we talked about in Step 5. This isn't so much about conflict as the everyday aggravations that happen to all of us. It's about welcoming that disturbance and developing the ability to be with the discomfort.

In her foreword to Bruce Tift's book *Already Free*, Sounds True publisher Tami Simon says, "Being able to commit to our disturbance when we are alone, perhaps on the meditation cushion or lying in bed, is one thing, but committing to disturbance in relationship, in my experience, is of a whole different order of magnitude."

Yes, it *is* easier in some ways to be alone, but for many of us, it isn't preferable—even with the increase in disturbances. Plus, disturbance happens in all of our relationships, not just the romantic, primary ones. One of the ways disturbance shows up in relationships is through the independence/connection polarity. This is a phenomenon in relationships in which each individual holds to the pole of independence or the pole of connection.

When one person holds the pole of independence, the other person has no choice but to hold the pole of connection, becoming dependent or needy. When someone holds the pole of connection, the other person has no choice but to move toward disconnection/independence. In fact, some couples hold to their own poles for the entirety of their relationship, battling with one another because of their differences. This is why opposites attract!

If I hold on to my pole of independence, I don't make room for the part of me that wants to trust and allow for some dependency in order to be more balanced. If I hold on to my pole of connection, I don't allow myself to explore independence.

Here's a description of these two "styles" of being:

Independence Style: This person overcompensates out of the core fears of suffocation and loss of self. This is stereotypically "masculine" energy, which has nothing to do with maleness but is all about energy. (Men and women hold both masculine and feminine energy.) This style's neurotic expression for the sake of self-preservation involves putting up a wall and becoming distant or unavailable. They don't want to acknowledge their codependency, so it becomes a shadow self. Then, when others express that codependent pole, independent types are triggered emotionally.

Connection Style: This person overcompensates out of the core fear of abandonment. It's stereotypically "feminine" energy. This style's neurotic expression for the sake of self-preservation involves becoming clingy and needy. They don't want to acknowledge their fear of abandonment, so it becomes a shadow self. Then, when others express fear of abandonment, connection types are triggered emotionally.

Then, there are those I call "swing state" people. They swing back and forth between one pole and the other, taking whichever one is unoccupied in the moment.

All of these styles are activated by our core wounding and our shadow beliefs. Neither pole is right or wrong. They just are. And our style is what we bring into our relationships. In my relationship with Aaron, for example, I'm the one who tends to hold the independence pole, while he holds the connection pole. The more I express my independence and desire for freedom, the more Aaron will dig in to his connection pole, demanding more closeness, and vice versa.

So what do we do? The goal is to let go of our fierce grasp on our respective poles and meet in the middle, in between the extremes. In this position, there's more equilibrium. I look for my version of connection, and Aaron looks for his version of independence. For example, he might say, "My version of independence shows up as feeling suffocated when you want to be chatty in the morning." I might say, "My version of connection is wanting you to come on one of my business trips with me." Believe me, it isn't always easy to find our "versions" of the other's experience, especially when we're fully polarized—him on the side of wanting more connection and me on the side of wanting more independence. But as hard as it may be, if we dig deep enough we can each find a way in which we can understand the opposite impulse.

As Aaron integrates more of his independent nature, I'll naturally begin to find the part of me that wants connection. As I integrate more of my ability to connect, Aaron will naturally gravitate toward wanting more separation. So even if one partner is willing to lean into the opposite pole, naming their version of whatever energy the other is expressing, the whole dynamic begins to shift. When we *both* lean into the pole of the other, we have an even better chance of achieving balance. It can be very powerful. It allows us to adopt the both/and approach of being both independent and dependent, rather than either/or. After all, each of us is both independent and dependent, even though we may tend to express one more than the other.

The more balanced place where we meet in the center is *interdependence*, which is mutual reliance on each other out of love rather than obligation. In a place of interdependence, we're each holding both energies and dancing between them. To cultivate this balance and reach a state of interdependency, independent people can work on their ability to allow support from their partner and open up to greater intimacy. They can begin to embrace "we-ness" as opposed to "I-ness." The connection types who naturally lean more toward dependency can work on self-reliance, learning to enjoy their own company and taking responsibility for their own needs rather than expecting someone else to care for them. Interestingly, dependent types usually need to open up to greater intimacy as well. This is because they tend to rely on others rather than develop intimacy with themselves. So the closeness they long for with others is elusive until they get to know their true selves better. (Take note, ye readers who are single and longing for connection!)

Of course, even when we get better at remaining interdependent, there will be times when we bounce to the pole that's our "go to"—the one we're most comfortable with. But if we stay aware, we can catch ourselves: "Oh, look, I've popped back to my pole, and he's bounced to his pole. I need to move myself back to center as best I can." This is its own type of "pole dance," which becomes an opportunity to negotiate differences rather than stay in opposition to each other.

The more aware we are of these inherent style differences, the less disturbed we'll be in relationships. But remember: Some disturbance is inevitable, and it doesn't mean there's something wrong with you or your relationship.

Exercise #19: Explore the Poles

How have the poles played out in your relationships? Let's find out. You probably already know whether you tend toward the Independent Style, the Connection Style, or swing state. If not, however, this exercise will help you determine your style.

1. Think about an intense argument you've had with a partner. Which of the poles did you

hold? Which pole did your partner hold? Write down what you can remember about how your adherence to your individual poles affected the argument.

Example: My wife and I argued about the fact that I never want to go with her to weddings. I hate weddings, but she feels abandoned if I refuse to go with her. Everybody asks her where I am, and she feels strange being there alone. I definitely held the independence pole in this argument, while my wife held the connection pole.

2. Think about another intense argument from your past—distant or recent. Did you adhere to the same pole as you did in the argument from number 1, or did you adhere to a different pole? Write down what you can remember about how your adherence to your individual poles affected this argument.

   Example: I was sick, and I wanted my wife to stay home with me rather than go to work. She had an important meeting that day and thought I was being a big baby. This turned into a big argument between us. In this instance, I definitely held the connection pole, while my wife held the independence pole.

3. If you tend toward one particular pole, can you recall a time when you flipped to the other one? If so, write down what you remember.

4. Choose one of the arguments you explored, and try to imagine how the conversation would have been different if you and your partner had attempted to move to center

rather than stay attached to your respective poles. Write down what you think would have happened.

Learning to Lean into Connection and Interdependence

For some reason, I have a lot of resistance about dancing. My ex-husband once told me I looked like Elaine in *Seinfeld* when I danced. If you've seen the show, you'll know what I mean. If you haven't, suffice it to say that she was probably the most embarrassing dancer in history.

To try to help me get over this resistance a few years ago, two friends took me to dance classes, and both times, I ended up crying in the parking lot.

Fast-forward to my relationship with Aaron. We were at a party in Aspen that included a live band, and Aaron asked me to dance. "Absolutely not," I said. But he asked again . . . and again . . . and again. So I finally gave in. We "sort of" danced, but it was traumatic for me once again.

Aaron could tell how difficult it was for me, so in his loving way, he suggested we take six weeks of dance classes together. Unfortunately, I still couldn't get past the trauma and ended up crying during the first two classes. "I'm not going back there again," I told Aaron.

Obviously, this trauma was locked inside my psyche, so Aaron and I decided to see a dance therapist. Aaron already knew the therapist, as did friends of mine. So I felt safe with her immediately. "This is my biggest nightmare," I told her. "I have a lot of resistance and fear about this, and I don't want to feel humiliated."

Luckily, this therapist was able to take us through a very slow process. She started by just having us move separately with our eyes closed. I could just be in my own world without being watched. With my eyes closed, I found that I could feel the music and let my body move the way it wanted.

Then, she had us do an exercise together called "The Seaweed Exercise." With our feet firmly planted on the ground, we took turns gently pushing each other's shoulders, causing our bodies to move like seaweed. It was so profound for me to be touched in this way and to move as if I was underwater. Aaron would also support my movement physically as I leaned into him.

Of course, everything that happens to us is a metaphor, so allowing Aaron to support me in this way also allowed me to "lean into" his pole of connection and balance my own independence pole a bit more. Since my long-running story is that no one will support me, it was beautiful to trust that he would support me through this movement, and I also began to release some of my trauma around dancing.

THE ENMESHMENT OF CODEPENDENCY

I've already covered how many of us put our own needs aside for everyone else, but those of us who do it habitually or to the extreme are what we call "codependent" types. Ironically, codependency is an effort to avoid disturbance and conflict, but it usually results in exactly that.

We stereotype codependency as weakness or as having to do with addiction. But it frequently happens in relationships where neither party is an addict. It's simply the act of allowing another person's behavior to determine our choices, actions, and behaviors. It's looking for someone outside of us to regulate us emotionally. This was my pattern in my marriage, so I know it well.

Codependent people "take on" the energy of others. Our boundaries are shaky, so consciously or unconsciously, we believe someone else's feelings are our feelings. We feel that what happens to them also happens to us. We all know what this looks like. We walk on eggshells, trying to make sure the other person is okay, while we forgo our own okay-ness. We wait to see if someone is in a good mood or bad mood to determine our own mood. We overstep our own boundaries and discount our own feelings and needs in order to take care of the other, to keep the peace, or to maintain our connection with that person. We might apologize when we're not actually sorry, tolerate cruel or even abusive behavior, and say we agree when we don't really agree. Inside, it's the desire to do whatever it takes to make the situation safe in our estimation.

It's connection at all costs, but the cost to self is great. We lose touch with our own autonomy, our own emotions, and our preferences. We become inauthentic, never giving our partner the gift of seeing who we really are.

This pattern often takes root in childhood, so you may have noticed it in your origin story. That's the case for my friend Alice, who became codependent as a result of her family environment. "My father's moods were so unpredictable," she says. "One minute, he was happy and smothering us with love. The next minute, he was going on a three-hour rant. So we always tiptoed around him, trying not to set him off. My mother's marriage was spent trying to keep him happy in order to just have a little peace. As a result, I've found that in relationships, my tendency has been to do everything I can to make my partner happy, whether or not I'm happy."

As my client Lily puts it, "I can see how my codependent survival techniques from childhood, trying to make my mother happy, have caused me to try to take responsibility for my partner's happiness, while destroying my own every time."

As codependents, we try to control as much as we can. We fear what might happen if we don't have control, so we do our kids' homework for them, for example, or treat our partner/spouse like a child rather than a lover, taking care of them excessively.

Ironically, we often feel *out of* control because we're trying so hard to control what we *can't* control. If we learn to "mind our own business," and only control what's actually within our power, we'll no longer feel so chaotic.

Mood-matching is another habit of codependent people, and it's so common that I'd also call it part of the old relationship blueprint. When we match moods with our partner, we feel like we're connected. But this is an unhealthy way to connect that doesn't honor our own individuality. Mood-matching is how we contain ourselves, make ourselves small, and end up feeling victimized. But with awareness, we can learn to stop doing it.

For example, let's say you wake up feeling great, but your partner is feeling down. To feel connected, you match your mood to your partner's and begin to feel down as well. Not only does this cause you to feel lousy, but it probably isn't helpful to your partner either, who might be more likely to come out of the negative space if you maintain your original positive mood.

It's mind-blowing for me that I can now stay anchored in my own mood regardless of Aaron's mood. For example, I'm a morning person. I'm chatty and full of smiles as soon as I wake up. Even though Aaron tends toward connection and likes to spend as much time with me as possible, he's the opposite of me in the morning. He needs coffee to get going and likes to sit with me quietly at first. Before I understood these differences between us, I interpreted his quietness as a bad mood and made it mean something about me. I thought, *What did I do wrong?* or *What do I need to do to fix his mood?*

A few months ago, he got up, came into the living room, got his coffee, and barely said hello or good-bye to me before he left the house. In the past, I would've come up with a whole story about what his behavior had to do with me. But thanks to many hours of couples' therapy and my own self-investigation, I was able to avoid falling into that old pattern this time. When I learned that mornings aren't Aaron's favorite time, I was able to let him be. Ten minutes after he left that day, he texted me to say that his alarm hadn't gone off, and he was late for an appointment. Turns out, his behavior had nothing to do with me. It wasn't personal. When we have a better understanding of our differences, we're less likely to take things personally that aren't actually personal.

Codependency is such an insidious dynamic in relationships that it can be challenging to isolate and shift it. My own tendencies never changed in my marriage but only began to shift during the divorce process. Releasing codependency is a matter of staying strong in our core and true to ourselves without allowing ourselves to be jarred by anything outside of us. We have to stand solid in our own feelings just like we've practiced in previous chapters.

Here's a radical thought: *We can still care about another person without "taking on" their emotions or problems.* For those of us who have been codependent for our entire lifetimes, this can be a difficult concept to grasp at first. We have to keep catching ourselves in the act of becoming enmeshed in our partner's (or any other person's) drama, and over time, we learn to detach. This doesn't mean we don't care about their pain anymore. It simply teases apart "caring about" and "sacrificing ourselves for." The former remains, while the latter is released.

The evolutionary journey to self-love and to a healthy relationship with another is a dance of dependence (relying on another), independence (self-reliance), codependence (enmeshed attachment that enables dysfunction), counter-dependence (refusal to attach), and interdependence (mutual reliance). While no one can maintain it 24/7, as I said in the previous section, interdependence is the healthiest way to be.

In an interdependent relationship, you take care of yourself, your partner takes care of himself/herself, and you rely on one another when it feels right to do so. It isn't about need, but about mutual—and neutral—reliance on each other. You shift from obligation to desire, so that you do things for each other because you genuinely want to. For those of us who have been codependent most of our lives, it takes some work to discern the difference.

Classic Codependency vs. High-Functioning Codependency

Some of us are the classic codependent type, frequently seen as "the doormat"—someone who gives and takes care of others excessively, almost never asking for what he/she wants.

Then there are those of us who are high-functioning codependents. That was me. We tend to be very capable and intelligent. We intellectualize our behavior, not realizing it's codependent, which we tend to see as weak. We're efficient and get a lot done, so we misinterpret our codependence as powerful. We see ourselves as achievers.

We're perfectionists and control freaks. Therefore, we infantilize our partner, insisting he/she isn't able to take care of most things properly. We have to do it ourselves to ensure it will get done the way *we* think it should be done. Then we feel victimized because we believe others are *making* us do everything. But we've actually volunteered to shoulder the burden, out of our perfectionism and control issues. And because our culture rewards perfection, we actually get positive reinforcement for our neurosis. It becomes a vicious cycle!

If this sounds like you, I urge you to begin to see your codependent habits and shift them. When you can relax your expectations and need to control, your partner and others in your life will, at least in time, become more self-reliant and appreciate your trust in them. And you'll stop feeling victimized and exhausted—an added bonus.

Exercise #20: How Solid Are Your Boundaries?

An emotional boundary is a limit that allows us to protect our own safety, dignity, and desires. Codependent people allow others to cross over these limits, or they cross their own by taking care of others more than taking care of themselves. Are you unsure if you're codependent? In this exercise, which consists of three parts, you'll answer some key questions to help you figure it out. Then we'll do a meditation to begin to dissipate codependency.

Part 1—Are You Codependent in Relationships?

Answer these questions about your tendencies in relationships:

1. Have you often felt you were the only one making an effort in your relationships?

2. Do you feel you don't have enough time for yourself?

3. Do you often feel that your partners and others in your life don't know how to accomplish tasks correctly or satisfactorily?

4. Do people in your life often rely on you to make plans and take care of details?

5. Have you ever found yourself stuck in a relationship, unable to break away emotionally?

6. Do you frequently hold back your feelings because you're afraid of hurting someone else or making them angry?

7. Do you struggle to let others know when they've hurt your feelings or done something insensitive?

8. Do you find it difficult to say "no" when someone asks you for help?

9. Do you often feel overwhelmed with all you've promised to do for others?

10. Do you believe it's courteous to let others make decisions, even when the decisions will affect you?

If you answered "yes" to any of these questions, you probably struggle with codependency to at least some degree.

Part 2—Strengthen Your Boundaries

If you began to assert your right to take care of your own needs, as we discussed in Step 6, you've already begun to set boundaries with your partner, family, friends, and/or co-workers. How else have you crossed, or allowed others to cross, your boundaries? How can you begin to set and hold better boundaries? For example, you may be the person in your household who's always expected to keep track of the schedule for everyone. What if you suggested to others that they begin keeping their own schedules?

Perhaps in the past you had a partner who crossed a boundary by saying mean things to you like, "Wow, you've put on some weight. Maybe you should skip that ice cream." You can decide that you won't tolerate such hurtful comments in your next relationship and work on loving yourself more in the meantime.

Write down a plan to strengthen your boundaries in any areas where they're weak. What can you do or say to stop allowing your boundaries to be violated? Set a particular date when you'll accomplish this. It might mean changing your own behavior or having a difficult conversation with someone in your life.

Part 3—Establish Specific Boundaries

If you need to establish a boundary with an adult who's very dependent on you, try this visualization. Imagine that you have a cord connecting your solar plexus, the flat area in the center of your torso between your bottom ribs, with the solar plexus of this person. This area is where your emotional chakra is located. Imagine what it would be like to cut that cord, and visualize (or feel, if you don't tend to "see" images) placing your loved one in the arms of his or her higher self—the wiser part of them that's connected to universal wisdom. Does it feel frightening to do this? Do you feel like you're abandoning this person?

This exercise is a way to begin to disengage from your attachment so that both of you can grow into the independent/interdependent people you're meant to be.

If the person who's dependent on you is your current partner/spouse, you can still do this exercise! It doesn't mean you're disengaging from them entirely. You're simply relinquishing your need to take care of them, while encouraging them to be more self-reliant.

CONFLICT NEGOTIATION VS. CONFLICT RESOLUTION

We've talked about cozying up to conflict and choosing authentic connection over trying to eliminate differences. This is another area that has been hard won for me. I've made a conscious choice to "lean in" during conflict or disturbance, when my impulse is to run. I've begun to trust that love isn't life-threatening, and that this relationship with Aaron has the resiliency to hold our differences and our truths. What I've discovered is that it's strong enough to contain the fullness of both.

One of the reasons for that strength is that we've made a commitment to conflict *negotiation* rather than *resolution*. In other words, if we can't come to an agreement right away, we negotiate rather than push until one of us acquiesces to the other's opinion. We honor the fact that we might never agree, and we find a way to cohabitate in spite of that.

As with all issues, the first step is to become more aware of what happens to you when conflict arises. Do you lash out or cower? Do you tend to feel more angry than afraid or vice versa?

My client Eleanor says she's noticed that she can become pushy and disrespectful of her partner's boundaries during arguments because she feels a need to pursue a resolution. She's now learning to let go of the need to settle all disagreements.

My client Emily says, "I've come to realize that I avoided being honest my whole life because it felt scary, when it's actually more frightening to not speak my truth because the consequences of not being honest are much worse. Now I'm beginning to see conflict as an opportunity to get to know myself and see where I've not been authentic. I can explore the insecurity or misconception behind the conflict."

Meanwhile, Michelle, who is currently single, is coming to terms with the fact that disturbance and conflict will always be there, in whatever relationship she's in. "I've begun to understand that triggers, discontent, and conflict are blessed signs of what's lost in me that needs to be healed," she says. "The beauty is choosing to understand it from a place of love, transformation, and opening rather than from a place of fear. Or a reason to shut down, control, or close off. It's a conscious decision to move toward self-reliance or mutual reliance rather than neediness or trying to control external outcomes."

Leah is beginning to change her attitude about conflict as well. "In the past, conflict meant winning and controlling—changing the other person to see it 'my way.' I either had to win the argument and change their opinion, or roll over and sacrifice myself," she says. "Now I see that it's about learning to let go of what doesn't matter in the end, and I've found that most of it is insignificant. I can stand up for what I believe in at the same time that I accept another opinion. I don't have to change them, and they don't have to change me. Now I ask myself if the conflict is truly a conflict or just my ego wanting to control things. I then ask myself if my stubbornness will make a difference in the situation at the end of the day, week, month, year, or lifetime. Usually not. I ask myself if a compromise means sacrificing my values. That's the determining factor. I won't sacrifice those, but I can still embrace another person's opinion because I now understand how our experiences and circumstances cause us to see the world in a way that differs from others."

What Leah says is key—we simply can't expect our partner to see everything the same way we do. No matter how compatible we may be, we're still two individuals who've grown up with different experiences and are bound to have different views from time to time. What we *can* do is learn how to be loving while being ourselves, which sometimes requires us to engage conflict in healthy ways.

STRATEGIES FOR CONFLICT NEGOTIATION

To move from resolution to negotiation when in conflict, Aaron and I have found that these strategies work well:

Get expert help. As I mentioned at the beginning of the chapter, Aaron and I started seeing a therapist as soon as we got back together. Now when our arguments become too emotionally charged, we push the proverbial "pause button." We recognize that we're suddenly swimming in the deep end without a lifeguard, so we table the issue until we can get help to prevent us from drowning. The "lifeguard" we've chosen is our therapist, Raven Wells. Aaron and I often joke that I'm speaking Chinese, and he's speaking Russian. Raven is the only person who seems to be able to translate for us.

What's fascinating is that we've built up enough trust—a strong enough container—that we can shift our emotional state and go on to make dinner, go for a walk, take time for ourselves, or even have sex after we've tabled a disagreement. We don't have to automatically invoke the silent treatment with one another, holding a grudge about the disagreement until the therapy appointment. We've learned to be compassionate with each other, and to stay in connection despite our conflict. (Obviously, this doesn't work if either party feels victimized or if anyone has been cruel or disrespectful during the argument. In that case, I believe you have only two options: either seek the professional help of a couples' therapist, counselor, or coach . . . or leave the relationship.)

See the other person's perspective. Remember my story about going to the other window, either literally or in my head, to get a new perspective? This technique helps a great deal. Put another way, it's about trying to step into our partner's shoes. Seeing the other person's side can be difficult to do, but it's a skill that can be developed. I'm still working on this particular skill! Aaron tends to be better at seeing my perspective than I am at seeing his. I still worry that if I acknowledge his point of view, I'll be forced to let go of mine and sublimate my needs. I've had to learn how to tune in to his way of thinking while honoring my own. It's a journey, but I'm here to tell you it's possible.

Relinquish the need to control, change, or fix the situation. This is easier said than done, but ultimately we have to come to terms with the fact that we don't necessarily know what's right or best. Actually, the unknown is where possibility lives, and where surprising options might become available to us.

My client Charles has been working on this one. "My biggest lesson from this work is that I don't need to force things to change or go the way I perceive they should," he says. "And then, the other big one is that I'm not going to change my wife. I'm going to be there to support her and give her space to change in the way she needs to change

. . . or not. There have been some huge challenges with her, and literally some breakdowns, but I've learned that if I just open my heart and say, 'I'm here to support you, hold you, and give you space,' the conflict eases more quickly, whether or not there's an actual resolution. Without this work, I would have stayed that person who felt I had to help her, change her, rescue her, or fix the situation."

Learn your partner's type in Love Language, the Enneagram, Myers-Briggs, PACT, etc. These personality-type tools can be very helpful for discovering why you and your partner differ from each other so much. (See the Resources section at the back of the book for a list of personality-type tools.) For example, in the language of Stan Tatkin, founder of the PACT Method (Psychobiological Approach to Couple Therapy), I'm an "Island" type. Islands hold the core belief that if we depend on another, our independence will be taken away, leaving us feeling robbed and trapped. This causes us to isolate ourselves.

Aaron, on the other hand, is a "Wave" type. Waves hold the core belief that they're going to be abandoned, so they're less independent and often cling to others. He's a "we" person, and I'm an "I" person. Based on the fact that my mom didn't attach to me right away, it's no wonder that "we-ness" doesn't come naturally to me.

In the past, when I started to long for solo time, I would freak out and revert to my old belief that I'm not built for relationship and should be alone. With the help of these personality-typing tools, I realized that I'm always going to need my alone time. There will always be moments when I feel suffocated. My "fight, flight, or freeze" muscle is going to get a workout for the rest of my life, and a part of me is going to find it annoying to share my life. The friction of rubbing up against another person will frustrate me at least some of the time, and I'm always going to project onto Aaron. But when I do, it isn't about him. It's about the mirror he holds up for me to see myself more clearly and to evolve.

That realization was huge for me because it means I don't have to be afraid when my "stuff" arises. I don't need to resist it or wish it would go away (or wish *he* would go away). I only need to listen to and honor the voice of my truth, knowing that my "stuff" is just an aspect of my personality.

Through Gary Chapman's work, *The 5 Love Languages*, we discovered that one of Aaron's key ways to communicate love is through giving gifts. According to Chapman, there are five ways we express love and feel loved, and we each have our preferences. When I took the Love Language test, unlike Aaron, I got a zero in the gifts category. They just don't matter to me.

Not long ago, Aaron gave me a donut pillow as a gift because I'd fallen while skiing and bruised my tailbone, which made sitting uncomfortable. The pillow was meant to improve my comfort. But since he gave it to me before we took the Love Language test, I fell into my old patterns immediately. I felt the gift insinuated that I can't take care of myself, which goes against my need to be independent, so it infuriated me. Once I discovered that one of his main love languages is gifts, I realized that what I made his gift mean had nothing to do with his intent. The meaning I'd made had everything to do with me, and nothing to do with who he was or what he intended. Once I recognized this, I softened about it and accepted the pillow with the affection it was meant to convey.

Once we know more about our own personality tendencies and those of our partner, we can be more accepting of our differences. Rather than taking our partner's behavior personally, we'll know that it's just an inherent part of who they are.

Then, even if we feel triggered, we can stop and evaluate what's truly happening in the moment, rather than indulging our knee-jerk response. Author and Holocaust survivor Viktor Frankl said, "Between stimulus and response there is a space. In that space is our power to choose our response. In our response lies our growth and our freedom." This space is where we have the opportunity to make a different, more conscious choice as to how we behave. That practice can help to dissipate a lot of conflict.

Now that you've honed your new skills, it's time to envision a healthy, interdependent relationship in which there is both love and freedom—that's what the next step is all about. But first, one last exercise.

Exercise #21: Personality Assessment Homework

Since this exercise isn't about writing your thoughts, it's more of a homework assignment.

Complete the 5 Love Languages quiz at http://www .5lovelanguages.com/profile/, and choose one more additional personality-type assessment to take. (See the Resources section on page 221 for my top picks.) If you're currently in a relationship, ask your partner to take these assessments as well. It can be a fun and enlightening way to connect and get to know each other better. And if you aren't in a relationship right now, taking these assessments will help you learn more about yourself and your own tendencies, preparing you for the next relationship when it comes along.

Relationship Reframe

"I strive for the balance of interdependence as I set healthy boundaries and become more comfortable with the inevitability of disturbance in relationships."

Step 9

Envision the Relationship You Desire

One of the reasons Aaron and I broke up for eight months is that he didn't want to be with someone who travels so much. He wanted someone who would go to sleep with him every night and wake up with him every morning. And he wasn't going to have that kind of relationship with me. Meanwhile, I had envisioned myself with a partner who liked to work and travel as much as I do. Someone who valued alone time as much as I do.

When we came back together after those eight months apart, we stopped trying to change each other.

Before our reconciliation, we focused on what *wasn't* working between us. When we agreed to try again, we made a concerted effort—with Raven's help—to focus on and maximize what *was* working in our relationship.

When we look for what's wrong in ourselves, our partner, or our relationship, we view our circumstances through a negative filter. This filter makes it easy to see imperfections, and it becomes a self-fulfilling prophecy, preventing us from seeing the good that does exist. When we look for what's right, on the other hand, we see the true value of our relationship.

So Aaron and I got real. We let go of our false belief that if *everything* isn't working, then *nothing* is. We don't deny the parts that don't work well; we simply accept them.

Human beings are imperfect. No one can be the ideal picture of everything we want, so for any relationship to work, a certain amount of acceptance is required.

Relationship isn't black and white; there's got to be room for nuance. That goes for all the advice in this book, by the way! Sure, I've suggested that you put yourself first. But that doesn't mean you refuse to negotiate or that *compromise* is a dirty word. There's plenty of room for nuance and plenty of room to accept the inevitable imperfections in your partner and your relationship.

At the same time, acceptance is different from being a doormat. It doesn't mean you accept abuse or misery, and it doesn't mean you abandon yourself. Each of us has our *nonnegotiables*—behaviors we simply can't tolerate or that are most important to us. (We're going to evaluate those in a moment.) But most of the day-to-day issues that arise in healthy relationships aren't as extreme as our nonnegotiables. And when it comes to everyday differences, the game plan includes acceptance, compromise, and negotiation.

Aaron still triggers me, of course . . . and vice versa. But each time, it's an invitation for me to come back to myself and examine those triggers. Again, they aren't about him; they're about me. As legendary psychologist Carl Jung said, "Everything that irritates us about others can lead us to an understanding of ourselves."

When Aaron behaves in a way I wish he wouldn't, I ask myself, "Can I accept this behavior, even if I don't like it?" Anything less causes me suffering. If I want the situation or Aaron to be different, that dissatisfaction will be painful for me. So my choices are to (1) get on board through acceptance, (2) attempt to negotiate/compromise with him about it, or (3) decide that the relationship isn't working for me.

Traveling, for example, is a nonnegotiable for me. For Aaron, having a partner who doesn't travel is a *preference*, rather than something he absolutely can't tolerate. So in order to be in relationship with me, he's made the choice to accept my frequent traveling, even if he doesn't like it.

The operative word here is *choice*. Each of us gets to decide if the cost of acceptance is too great, if important boundaries are being crossed, or if it's tolerable. Is it worth breaking up over? Or is it worth compromising to keep the relationship intact? When you hold firm to something you know upsets your partner, what does it cost you? Is the issue a nonnegotiable or more of a "good to have"? There's a balance to be achieved.

Are your desires for the relationship being mostly satisfied—or not? Is the relationship enhancing your life, or providing you with little or nothing? Is the relationship making your life easier or harder? Remember that it's your job to take care of your needs, but that doesn't mean you get *nothing* from your partner.

On the other hand, if you think your relationship is making your life worse, stop to evaluate whether your life would truly improve if the relationship ended. Is the problem really the relationship and this particular partner, or will you have the same issues alone or in the next relationship—because they're *your* issues?

As we discussed in Step 6, you have a choice as to what kind of relationship you create. So it's important to have a "vision" for that relationship. It might be difficult, however, to let go of what you think a relationship "should" look like in order to develop the vision of what will truly work for you. That was the case for my client Grace.

"We had a similar situation to Nancy's," she says. "My partner works a ton and travels a ton. That rubbed up against my ideal that says 'I need to see you every day.' So we split up."

When they got back together, both had evolved. "We lived together for a couple of years, but now he has his own home. It conflicts with my cookie-cutter fantasy ideal, but it's working." Grace is beginning to see that it isn't necessary to be together all the time in order to have a satisfying relationship.

For you, such an unconventional setup might be a nonnegotiable, an absolute no—which is fine! The beauty of it is that you get to choose what a fulfilling relationship means to you. I'm simply suggesting that you do it without the pressure of societal norms. Like Grace, be honest enough to figure out what truly works for you.

Leah is single right now, but her vision for the relationship she wants has also changed significantly since working with the new relationship blueprint. "I was surprised how my new vision differs from what I assumed relationships were supposed to be—married, self-sacrificing, having to choose between dominant or submissive. I'm more open than I realized. It's about what brings me joy and harmony. It's much more of a give and take with some compromise, but without losing myself. It's also awareness that I'm fine with whatever the future holds. I'm not concerned with what others may think, or anxious about what has to happen in a specific time period."

It all starts with clarity of vision, which is the gravitational force that governs change. Once you're clear on that vision, you'll be motivated to make the choices and take the actions that will help you achieve it rather than choices that sabotage you. Change happens in a particular sequence—vision, then choice, and then action.

If you're single, your vision will help you make different choices about the people you date. If you're in a relationship, you and your partner will hopefully work together to clarify what you want so that you can co-create it. And yes, you and your partner need to have a similar vision for your relationship to work.

Let me be clear: I'm not talking about magical thinking or manifesting here. I'm talking about rolling up your sleeves and *crafting*—co-creating with your partner—the relationship you want. This is a balanced approach, which I acknowledge can be challenging. On the one hand, you're working to make sure your needs are met. On the other hand, you're trying to be realistic about relationships and about your partner. You don't want to create a vision from the fairy-tale prince/princess myth (which is, actually, a kind of magical thinking). At the same time, you have the right to craft the relationship you want. I would just urge you to investigate your desires carefully. Again, are you asking something from your partner that, upon consideration, you must actually fulfill for yourself?

My client Claire recently met with an old friend who said, "Are you happy in your relationship?" Claire responded, "My new relationship blueprint doesn't depend on my relationship for happiness." She says that in the past, she depended on a relationship to make her happy, but now it's an "add-on" to her feelings of fulfillment.

So Step 9 is about empowering yourself to co-create the future relationship you want, whether it's a new version of your current relationship or one with a brand-new partner. We'll figure out your nonnegotiables and talk about the importance of surrender and getting comfortable with uncertainty. Then, you'll move on to envision the best relationship for you.

Exercise #22: Determine Your Nonnegotiables

This exercise is in three parts. First, you'll evaluate your values, which will help you with Parts 2 and 3—creating two lists of nonnegotiables. One list is behaviors you won't tolerate or must have in yourself, and the other is behaviors you won't tolerate or must have in a partner. When you're clear what you're available for and what you're not available for, you can avoid a great deal of stress and anxiety. You and your partner can then ask, "What are we available for together?"

If you and your partner or potential partner both write down your nonnegotiables, you'll have an idea if you're compatible. Remember that nonnegotiables are not what you'd "like" to have. These are behaviors you absolutely won't tolerate or absolutely must *have. When you explore your vision in the next exercise, you'll explore what you'd* like *to have.*

Part 1—Your Core Values

Determining your nonnegotiables and your relationship vision might be easier if you think about your values—what you value most in life. What's truly important to you? When we haven't thought about what matters most to us, our choices are haphazard. Knowing the values we hold most dear allows us to make informed choices. We can evaluate every situation based on these values. For example, if honesty is very important to you, a relationship with someone who's frequently dishonest won't work.

Here's a short list of some possible values that might top your own list, but feel free to think of your own. While all of these might be important to you in some respect, choose no more than five that are *most* significant for you. This will help you pinpoint what we'll call your "core" values.

Abundance	Honesty
Communication	Humor
Compassion	Independence
Connection	Inspiration
Courage	Integrity
Creativity	Intimacy
Excellence	Intuition
Family	Loyalty
Flexibility	Passion
Freedom	Respect
Friendship	Romance
Fun	Self-Expression
Growth	Self-Love
Happiness	Spirituality
Health	Success

Part 2—Nonnegotiables in Yourself

Now that you have a better idea of your values, let's pin-point your nonnegotiables.

Make a list of five or more nonnegotiables—behaviors that you won't tolerate or that you must have *in yourself* to feel satisfied by your relationship. Here are some examples from my clients:

"I must have the time and space for myself that I desire."

"I must go to sleep and wake up on a schedule that suits me."

"I will not tolerate any more rescuing of others; I can't save anyone. I'll simply support them in a way that doesn't compromise my own happiness as they solve their own problems."

"I must take responsibility for myself and work

through my issues as they arise."

"I choose to believe I'm worthy of love no matter what."

Part 3—Nonnegotiables in Your Partner

Next, make a list of five or more nonnegotiables— behaviors that you won't tolerate or must have in your partner:

"I won't allow passive-aggressive communication or verbally abusive words."

"I won't tolerate physical abuse."

"Honesty is an absolute."

"I must have a partner who's willing to work on his own issues and not rely on me to take care of his needs."

"We allow each other space to be alone and creative."

THE WISDOM OF SURRENDER

In my relationship with Aaron, I don't have everything I want, but I have more than I had in my marriage. And since I'm the common denominator in all of my relationships, I'm well aware that the grass isn't greener anywhere else. So I take care of my own needs and make sure I have my nonnegotiables, while I accept most everything else.

Yes, I have a vision of the kind of relationship I want, but it's important that my relationship vision isn't so rigid or such an image of perfection that it's unattainable.

There's wisdom in acceptance. Another word for that is *surrender*. Once we know our nonnegotiables, we can release our willful stronghold that things need to be a certain way, giving ourselves permission to want what we want, while also being okay with the reality of "what is."

The caveat, of course, is that we don't surrender those nonnegotiables! If we do choose to negotiate one of those, it must come from a conscious, self-loving place. It can't be out of fear of losing the relationship, because our partner demands it, or out of some sense of obligation. That wouldn't be a self-loving choice.

Knowing what to accept in our partner and what not to accept, what to surrender and what not to surrender, can be difficult. It requires awareness and discernment. We simply do the best we can in each moment and continue to evolve, learning more about ourselves and evaluating our decisions regularly. Ultimately, it comes down to self-worth because if we love ourselves enough, we won't accept behavior from others that isn't loving to us.

When we demand that our relationships have to be a certain way *beyond our nonnegotiables*, however, or when we demand that our partner act in a certain way, we're resisting what is. Positive change happens when we stop resisting and surrender to the reality of the situation.

This could mean that you and your partner come to a better understanding and improve your relationship, or it could mean that you end your current relationship. If you're single, it means that you stop resisting not yet having a relationship. You surrender to your singlehood, even if that means also surrendering to loneliness.

Try this: Tighten all the muscles in your body for a moment. Then take a deep breath, and release. You've just had a tangible experience of resistance followed by surrender.

Whatever we refuse to accept causes internal resistance and suffering. We can resist circumstances, people, behaviors, conditions, and even thoughts or beliefs. As long as we make them wrong or wish they were different than they are, we're resistant to what is.

Again, there's nuance here. Accepting what is doesn't mean we're giving up or throwing in the towel. If you choose to speak up and ask for what you want, you aren't resisting. If you walk away from a relationship or situation that isn't loving to you, you aren't resisting. In those cases, you're taking positive action.

If you stay in that relationship or situation without speaking up for yourself, however, wishing it to be other than it is, you're resisting what is. If you complain without taking action on your own behalf, you're resisting. If you refuse to accept that your relationship and your partner will never be perfect, you're resisting.

Resistance is a protective mechanism. It can act as an emotional shield that we unconsciously (or sometimes consciously) put up to guard ourselves against fear or pain. The problem, though, is that resistance can't protect us from hurt. Instead, it binds us to the emotional pain of the situation. It's the glue that keeps the pain sealed in and keeps us mired in the circumstances that we most dislike.

Remember Carl Jung's famous line that I mentioned earlier in the book: "What you resist persists." Resistance to what is keeps us stuck in the conditions of the past and prevents us from moving forward in our lives. When we're in any way attached to the idea that things are not as they should be, we're in resistance, going against the natural flow of life. It's like swimming in a swiftly moving river and struggling to go upstream. It's exhausting. Can you think of any circumstances in your life for which that's true right now? Maybe even in your current or most recent relationship?

When we're experiencing pain in a relationship, or especially during a separation or breakup, it's common to slip into resistance. We might have decided that the other person was wrong or unfair. We want the situation to be different from what it is. We hold on to our self-righteous position in an effort to defend and protect our hurt feelings, unfulfilled expectations, and unrealized dreams. We become attached to our beliefs and opinions about how it *should* have been out of fear that we'll never get what we want.

We resist, feeling that if we let go and surrender, our life will be out of control. But resistance is the number-one culprit that prevents us from healing and moving on. How many people resist getting a divorce, preferring to stay in an uncomfortable situation rather than risk stepping into the unknown? They make excuses for their partner's disrespectful behavior, resisting the truth that the relationship doesn't honor who they are. I know that one well!

Remember: Surrender doesn't in any way mean we've lost or that we're weak. It means we're moving *with* the flow of our life circumstances and not against it. We trust that every experience—even the most painful ones—are there for us to learn and grow.

In my training with Debbie Ford, I learned that surrendering to circumstances as they exist is an act of courage that calls on us to have faith in the unknown. And ironically, we open up to love more when we surrender our fear of not being loved. Then we don't hold so tightly to a love that may no longer serve us, so that we can open to the possibility of something better. We can welcome our vision for a new kind of relationship.

Exercise #23: Meditation on Resistance

This meditation will help you discover what you're resisting, as well as the fears underneath that resistance. It can be an emotional meditation, but you're ready!

Be sure to turn off all phones so that you can surrender to this process. Sit on a comfortable chair or couch in comfortable clothes. Feel free to play soft music or light candles, if you like. It helps to record your own voice reading the steps so that you don't have to open your eyes, which will disrupt your meditative state. You may wish to skip the italicized portions of the meditation when you record.

1. Close your eyes, and take several breaths. Relax each part of your body, starting with your feet. Then, gradually move up your legs, hips, belly, chest, back, arms, neck, and head until you feel fully relaxed. *Don't work too hard at this. Just ask your body to relax. As you continue, it will relax more and more.*

2. Feel yourself go deep within, and ask yourself this question: "What aspects of my current relationship or singlehood do I most resist?" It's something that has driven you to deny, struggle with, and hold on to the past, or otherwise fight the flow of life.

3. As you sit in the safety of your internal world, allow yourself to feel this resistance to your current circumstances.

4. Take another breath, and ask yourself, "What am I holding on to? What person, situation, or feeling have I not wanted to let go of? What has holding on cost me?" Has it cost you joy, self-respect, dignity, freedom, or something else? Allow yourself to see what

you've given up, missed out on, or been unable to achieve due to holding on to your resistance and fear.

5. Next, ask yourself, "What would be available to me if I let go? What action can I take this week that will support me in letting go and surrendering my resistance and fear?" Then, write down what action you will take, and commit to that action this week. *You might decide to meditate on it, write in your journal about it, or write an affirmation, mantra, or power statement 20 or more times each day.*

GET COMFORTABLE WITH UNCERTAINTY

Just as we need to become more comfortable with disturbance and surrender to what is, we need to relax a bit around the inevitability of uncertainty. There's much we can't control in this life. So the more we learn to trust that life's experiences are here to teach us important lessons, the more we can let love come and go.

As someone who clung to a marriage long after its "expiration date," trust me when I say I know how hard this is! But the kind of love we're talking about in the new relationship blueprint is the kind that—come what may—we don't grasp out of desperation or fear.

We actually have to learn how to release our need for certainty to have this kind of *alive* love that's based on truth. But guess what? It's much, much, much easier when we love ourselves and know that our "primary partner"—*me*—is never leaving.

As difficult as it is, we need to be willing to close doors in order to open new ones. We need to step into the unknown. Yet, uncertainty in and of itself may not be a reason to leave a relationship. Often people think that uncertainty, or that other very human feeling—loneliness—means something's wrong with them, their partner, or the relationship. This is when we're required to evaluate the situation with awareness to determine if we truly need to break up. Or are we just buying into the belief that the grass is greener because we want to escape the inevitable uncertainty and loneliness that most of us feel?

Accepting uncertainty also means we're willing to say, "I don't know." Maybe you aren't sure right now if you should stay or leave a relationship. In that case, be willing to admit that you don't yet know how to fix your situation. You may need to give yourself more time to make the best choice, or you may need to get counsel from a professional.

The stories we tell ourselves are there, in no small part, to give us a false sense of certainty. If we begin to let go of those stories, we can approach each moment of friction in the relationship with curiosity rather than defensiveness. Then we can allow for something new to unfold. We can even accept the possibility that we don't know our partner as well as we thought, and we don't know ourselves as well as we thought. We can be pleasantly surprised if we're not always looking through the lens of what we believe we already know.

By doing this, we eliminate the false belief in familiarity that often makes relationships grow stale. We acknowledge that knowing our partner "so well" that he/she becomes boring is nothing more than an illusion.

Since all of us are constantly evolving, I recommend allowing your partner and relationship to be different from what you thought/believed they were. And let them be more than you thought/believed they were. Permit the relationship to be its own entity that unfolds in its own way. Be willing to relinquish the patterns you've fallen into and make room for something greater. This is how you lean into loving your life and accepting the inevitability of uncertainty. When you do that, you allow your life to evolve naturally, without insisting that your future show up like your past in order to feel comfortable. That kind of comfort, which doesn't allow for healthy change, will only cause your growth to stagnate.

THE OLD BLUEPRINT VS. THE NEW BLUEPRINT

You now have a list of your nonnegotiables, and you've explored the importance of surrender and getting comfortable with uncertainty. Next, you're going to create your vision for the relationship you'd like to have. To prepare for that, let's revisit some of the tenets of the new relationship blueprint that we've discussed throughout the book. That way, as you work on your vision, you'll recall the principles that make for a healthier partnership.

The old blueprint said "the needs of the other come first." The new blueprint says "self-love comes first." I will ask myself what I want before I automatically try to make everything okay for the other person.

The old blueprint told us our own needs had to collapse for the sake of the relationship. The new blueprint says that loss of self is unhealthy for any relationship, and we don't have to lose ourselves at all. We can give ourselves what we need while also contributing to a loving, intimate, connected partnership with someone else.

With the old relationship blueprint, we assumed something was wrong if our partner didn't meet our needs. It was easier to believe we just hadn't found the right person. Or we thought we could have the perfect relationship *if only* he/she would change . . . or *if only* we could be better or do better . . . or *if only* we were worthy of the perfect person.

With the new relationship blueprint, we recognize that filling our own needs is our job, and our partner's needs are his/her job. Our relationship enhances our lives, but it doesn't fill empty spaces that only we can fill for ourselves.

According to the old blueprint, when we needed or wanted something that caused our partner to feel uncomfortable (or vice versa), we were labeled as selfish. We believed we were responsible for taking care of the needs of each other, which was an impossible task.

The new relationship blueprint means that our partner might need something that causes us to feel uncomfortable, or vice versa. But since we're now each taking care of our own needs, we can create a container in which conflict and discomfort can be endured. We understand that disturbance is to be expected and that it doesn't have to be a threat to the relationship. We can often allow our partner what he/she needs, even if it isn't our preference, and vice versa.

One of the causes of friction in relationships is wanting the other person to behave in a certain way that's unrealistic because it isn't in keeping with where our desires overlap. Since the old relationship blueprint never allowed us to discuss our desires in the first place, we made assumptions without any honest communication. And since we assumed, based on the old blueprint, that the other person was supposed to take care of our needs, we blew a lot of small issues out of proportion. The fact that our partner didn't want to go with us to a party became attached to a belief that he/she wasn't taking proper care of us or that it meant he/she didn't love us. In many cases, it only meant that our partner preferred to skip the party. Under the new blueprint, we can allow our partner to honor herself/himself, even if it means we'd rather they come to the party with us. This is acceptance.

With the old blueprint, we felt we had to hide ourselves in order to be loved by our partner. With the new blueprint, we know we have to be authentic with our partner in order to be true to ourselves and to feel loved for who we truly are.

Under the old blueprint, intimacy was about the *quantity* of time we spent together. Under the new blueprint, intimacy is about the *quality* of the time we spend together—time in which we're fully present with each other rather than wishing we were somewhere else.

The old blueprint said we had to be in a couple in order to feel whole and fulfilled. It told us a relationship would save us and that it would be our everything—the old "you complete me" syndrome. The new blueprint says we may choose to be in a couple to enhance our life, but not to fulfill it. We know that a relationship with someone else can't save us, and making our relationship *everything* is too much pressure to put on it. Instead of "you complete me," we adopt "you complement me."

With the old blueprint, we believed conflict meant the relationship was in trouble or we'd chosen the wrong partner. We believed every disagreement had to be resolved, and we felt unsafe if we didn't ultimately prove we were "right."

With the new blueprint, we know that relationship in and of itself is irresolvable; conflict is to be expected, and connection is more important than resolution. We recognize that if we disagree, no one in the relationship is necessarily right or wrong. (This, of course, assumes your partner isn't abusive.)

Under the old blueprint, we got into relationships for a number of reasons, including to have children. Under the new blueprint, we see relationship as a spiritual path—an opportunity for growth and healing. In my relationship with Aaron, healing is the major theme. It's actually comforting that we've come together for the purpose of reparation, restoration, and integration. Our relationship is really an accelerated Ph.D. program for learning about *me*. And for him, it's his own Ph.D. program for learning about himself.

The old blueprint said our relationship should follow the norm. The new blueprint says our relationship can be whatever works for the two of us.

Now that you've reviewed the principles of the new relationship blueprint, it's time to set your own vision of relationship. I suggest you go for broke in your vision, within reason. Remember that this is an "ideal" based on the new relationship blueprint, not the old one that was largely based on a myth. This isn't about Prince or Princess Charming, and it isn't about creating a vision that's unattainable. State what you want in your vision. Just know that once you're in a relationship, some surrender will be necessary; no person or relationship is perfect, and there will always be a degree of uncertainty, no matter how clear your vision may be.

Exercise #24: Setting Your Vision

This exercise is in two parts. In Part 1, you'll formulate a vision of your ideal relationship—a desired set of conditions and circumstances.

In Part 2, you'll explore what choices and actions you need to take in order to make your vision a reality.

Please read through the entire exercise before beginning.

Part 1—Your Highest Vision of Relationship

1. Close your eyes and bring to mind the highest vision you have for relationship. It's your vision in terms of communication, intimacy, difference, disturbance, conflict, and connection. To form the vision, ask yourself these questions:

   • What would I like to feel in relationship?

   • What do I need in order to be happy, satisfied, and fulfilled in my relationship?

   • What's the value of a romantic relationship for me?

   • Now that I know a relationship isn't about perfection, saving me, or finding someone to fill all of my needs, how does a relationship fit into my life?

2. If you're struggling at all to come up with your new vision, refer back to Exercise #7 in Step 3 when you excavated your underlying commitments. The answer you gave to #4 in Part 3 ("New Commitments"), in which you envisioned how your life and relationships would be different with your new commitment in place, might be helpful.

3. Next, write down your vision so that you don't forget it. It might take the form of random thoughts, a story, a recipe, or just images that you see or feel in your mind. Here's an example from one of my clients:

   "My highest vision for a relationship is one

with a strong connection. If it was a diagram, it would be two overlapping circles. Each of us is strong in our own sense of self, feelings, goals, hopes, dreams, and ability to care for ourselves. The overlap is where the relationship creates itself. This space is open for the other to enter. It's kind and accepting, not judgmental. It's curious and seeks understanding. As the positive connections continue, the relationship strengthens. The relationship is part of who we are as individuals, even when we're not together. We don't have to come together at all times because the connection can span thousands of miles and stay strong. Mutual sexual chemistry and desire are undeniable, and the stronger our connection and understanding, the stronger the desire. Most importantly, this is a relationship about support, not compromise. It's one in which we're both whole before we become even better together."

Part 2—Choices and Actions to Create Your Vision

Answer these questions about choices and actions related to your vision. Again, be sure to write down your answers! Then come back to these questions periodically to think of new insights.

1. What choices and actions have you made thus far in relationships that have moved you away from your vision?

   Example: I've expected my relationships to fulfill me. I've wanted my partner to be my everything. When he wasn't able to be, I thought it meant something was wrong. Then, I'd leave the relationship, looking for the next one that might fulfill me. As an action, I've complained when my partner didn't take care of me in the way I should have been taking care of myself.

2. What new choices and actions will you take to replace the ones from the past that haven't served you?

    Example: In my next relationship, I don't want to expect my partner to be my everything or take care of me. I want him to be a companion and lover, not a rescuer. So I won't complain if he doesn't live up to all of my expectations, and I'll work through disagreements with him rather than cut and run.

3. What new actions will you take to make your vision a reality? What do you need to do within yourself? What do you need to do with your partner for your vision to come to fruition?

    Example: Right now, while I'm single, I'm going to work on learning how to fill my own needs rather than rely on anyone else. To make my vision a reality, I need my next partner to be on board with the new relationship blueprint.

    Example: I will ask my partner to create his/her vision. Then we'll come together and see if we can agree on a mutual vision that we can co-create together. (Note that this is another situation in which you may need a professional therapist, counselor, or coach to help the two of you negotiate your vision.)

4. If you're single, what choices and actions will cultivate your vision in preparation for a new person in your life?

   Example: I will try my vision on for size every day in my mind during my shower. That way, it won't take extra time. As the water rushes over me, cleansing me of the past, I'll see myself with my partner, having the kind of relationship I envision, where we complement each other in a healthy way.

5. If you're currently in a relationship, what can you do to cultivate your vision so that your relationship can transform?

   Example: I plan to discuss the new relationship blueprint with my wife. I'm going to ask her if she can join me in no longer expecting so much of each other. I'm also working on my emotional triggers so that I'm not so reactive with her, and I plan to work on balancing my tendency to hold the independence pole so much.

RELATIONSHIP 2.0

With this step comes very good news: You now have the tools to co-create a wonderful relationship with your partner based on the new relationship blueprint! It's Relationship 2.0. Again, this may mean creating a brand-new relationship, or creating a "new" relationship within your current one. Jungian analyst Marion Woodman has said that she and her husband had several marriages within their one marriage. If we're flexible enough, we can reinvent ourselves and re-create our relationship based on who we are today.

My client Anna has done that with her partner. They got divorced, lived together under the same roof to coparent, and then remarried. "I'm coming to the relationship in such a new way that it's really good, rich, fun, and silly. And it's all the things we had many, many years ago—like many marriages ago," she says.

Sophia is ready for Relationship 2.0. She's finished trying to live by normal conventions. "I no longer feel like I'm supposed to meet all these 'demands' that come with being married just because that's what other women do in relationships," she says. "And because they don't know how to voice their needs, their health declines, or they numb out of their lives through various addictions. I truly feel like the ceiling of my life has slid away. I can see the stars in the sky. I no longer feel trapped by the social confines I grew up with. Just because I'm not like most people doesn't mean something's wrong. It means I'm more tuned in. It's a strength, not a weakness."

As my client Peter is working on creating Relationship 2.0 with his wife, he asked me how you make a request of your spouse without being needy. "You *are* needy," I told him. "You're both needy *and* self-reliant like all of us. There's no point in hiding it."

He wanted to ask his wife for more time together so that they could deepen their connection and communication. I suggested he make his request in this way: "In order to honor our relationship, I want to see if you have interest in teaming up with me to schedule uninterrupted time together. I'd love to deepen our connection and communication."

Now, I know that negotiation and clear communication doesn't always work, and sometimes our visions and nonnegotiables are incompatible with our partner's. It isn't my intention to cause breakups, but if your current relationship truly doesn't work, you may indeed need to move on. My only wish for you is that you have the most fulfilling life possible, whatever that means for you, and that you continue to learn and evolve.

The new relationship blueprint also has the potential to make breakups go more smoothly. Obviously, I can't guarantee that; a lot depends on your partner. But my client Claire has used these principles and, as a result, went through a recent breakup that was very mature. The two of them were separated for a while and then explored the possibility of reuniting. They still care about each other and both understand that no one is to blame.

"We discussed endings and how that would look," she says. "And then we discussed what staying together would look like with new boundaries and the new blueprint. Then, he said, 'I really love you, but right now, I just love myself a little bit more. I have you to thank because I watched you evolve, and you left me alone for a long time. I had to find my way.' The old me would've been so threatened by what he said, but I realize that both of us need to focus on ourselves right now. So I don't know what the future looks like, but our discussion was so freeing for me."

What if you're dating or getting ready to date? How do you bring your new vision to the table? Well, maybe you leave it at home for the first couple of dates. It could overwhelm even the most evolved person. But once the relationship is moving in a serious direction, I highly recommend beginning to talk about what you envision. I know someone who proposed to his now wife by putting his most important possessions on the floor. There were his guitar, his journals, and his bike. He told her more about who he is and asked, "This is me. Do you think you can live with all of these parts of me?"

With the tools you've gathered in these chapters, you have the opportunity to navigate through the disturbances and conflicts that inevitably come up in relationships. You'll be more likely to catch yourself when you start to tell yourself a false story about what those disturbances and conflicts mean. You'll also have a better sense of what you want and what you won't tolerate, what to accept and what to surrender. Then, you'll be able to negotiate with your partner to create what you envision.

In the book *Creating Union*, author Eva Pierrakos puts it brilliantly. "When two equals relate," she writes, "both carry the full responsibility for the relationship. This is indeed a beautiful venture, a deeply satisfying state of mutuality. The slightest flaw in a mood will be recognized for its inner meaning and thus the growth process is kept up. Both will recognize their co-creation of this momentary flaw—be it an actual friction or a momentary deadness of feelings. . . . This will largely prevent injury to the relationship."

One of the side benefits of the new relationship blueprint is that it doesn't just help us create better romantic relationships. It also has the potential to improve our friendships, as well as relationships with co-workers and family members. Sophia has experienced this with her mom. "She comes from the old relationship blueprint and the belief that work outside the home is the man's role. I shared the new blueprint with her, and she thought it was amazing. We ended up having one of the deepest conversations we've had maybe in my whole adult life. I didn't expect her to react that way. She said, 'Oh, my God, where was Nancy when I was growing up?' She asked me lots of questions. So a beautiful offshoot of this work is that my mom and I had the best Mother's Day we've ever had."

Leah says, "All of my relationships have changed—family, work, co-workers, friends, and even 'relationships' in traffic. I'm not in an intimate relationship at the moment, but I can see myself in a healthy one soon. I'm much calmer and more relaxed. Little things don't bother me, and if something comes up, I have the tools available to work through it without involving someone else. I don't let others' moods bring me down or automatically think I did something wrong to ignite them. I have no anxiety going out by myself or meeting new people. I don't project what 'might happen,' and I don't need to be right all the time. I've let go of things always having to be my way, yet I'm also standing strong in my core values."

Bear in mind, though, that the pull of the old blueprint—and your old way of being—will no doubt be strong. Once you've found yourself, it takes vigilance not to lose yourself again. It's like building a muscle at the gym, except you're working on your relationship and your life instead of your body. And you'll need to forgive yourself when you fall short of your own expectations.

Are you excited about the possibilities and about your vision? Let's distill the details of your vision down to a single power statement that will support you as you create it. Because this statement is shorter, you can commit it to memory and think about it during the course of your day. You might want to write it repeatedly like an affirmation or make it into a beautiful picture that you can put on your wall. It's up to you.

Let's call it your "Relationship 2.0 Mantra." Mine is "I have more than enough room for love in my life." What's yours?

EXERCISE #25: YOUR RELATIONSHIP 2.0 MANTRA

In this exercise, you'll create a power statement to support your vision of the relationship you want.

Take a look at the vision you wrote down in Part 1 of Exercise #24. What's the bottom line—the most important thing you want for yourself in relationship?

Here are some of my clients' Relationship 2.0 mantras to give you some ideas:

"It is safe for me to love and be loved while we both are accepting, authentic, and balanced."

"First me. Then you."

"Loving another does not mean losing myself."

"I gracefully embrace access to both/and instead of either/or."

"Everything is working out for my highest good. It's safe to be me, it's safe to be you, it's safe to be we."

"My relationships are deeply connected, loving, honest, and whole."

"I am open to creating authentic connection and spiritual intimacy with a like-minded partner."

Now write your own Relationship 2.0 mantra, and post it somewhere you can see and repeat it every day.

Relationship Reframe

"I co-create a relationship based on my values and the knowledge that no one can make me whole but me."

Step 10

Lean into Love

I choose to stay with Aaron because the relationship serves my growth, not because I *need* anything from him. What I receive are yummy things that I *want* because they enhance my life—an opportunity for growth, love, friendship, companionship, spiritual awakening, healing . . . and great sex, just to name a few. But it's all still icing on the cake—a cake I've made for myself.

For me, *leaning into love* means, first and foremost, that I put myself first, trusting that Aaron is an adult who can take care of himself (except, perhaps, when he goes and breaks his collarbone). Yes, I make conscious time for the two of us to be fully present with each other, and I've learned how to put everything else aside for those commitments. But we both recognize that we're individuals. Though we're in a relationship, we aren't "one." It's counterintuitive, but leaning into self-love is precisely what has allowed me to lean further into my love for Aaron.

Yet I'm still clear that in the end, my "happily ever after" story is with myself.

When we understand that we are our own princes and princesses—our own rescuers—we stop looking for someone else to do that for us. We might even resist the endings of relationships a bit less. We can weather the storms within relationships better, too—like my client Sophia.

"I started working with Nancy not knowing if I'd stay married to my husband for another month," she says. "After just a few weeks, it dawned on me that the man I am with now is the type of guy I'd want to meet and have in my life if I were to reenter relationship down the road. Yes, he had an affair 15 years ago. Yes, he broke my trust. Yes, it broke my heart and brought me to my knees. Yes, it's been rough living with that since he told me about it six years ago. I'm not going to candy-coat it because it really does suck that he did that.

"However, with all of that blowing up in my face, I was forced to become the love of my own life—even though I didn't want to be. I now see how easily I put my worthiness in the hands of others. By falling in love with myself and allowing myself to grow, I can unfreeze my husband from that moment in time. I don't like it when others freeze me in time, so why perpetuate it on others? Especially my partner. As of this moment, we're doing much better. Our talks are supportive and clear. I think we both feel the release of old paradigm thinking as we move together in support of me, him, and us."

Falling in love with herself helped Sophia to heal and reestablish trust and connection with her husband. As singer-actress Eartha Kitt (who played Catwoman on the *Batman* TV show in the 1960s) once said, "I fall in love with myself, and I want someone to share it with me. I want someone to share *me* with *me*." Yes! This is healthy. This is the goal.

As I said at the beginning of the book, when self-worth/self-love is missing, we can't feel the love coming in from the outside even when it's available. The love can't land unless it's already growing inside of us. Again, it's like we don't have a port for that cord. So even if a great person comes along, we can't accept it. We secretly don't believe we deserve them. Unconsciously, we find fault with the person, and we cut and run. Then we make up stories about how love isn't available to us. And it's true that love isn't available to us, because we aren't giving it to ourselves.

It's a kind of self-abandonment. So many of us do exactly as I did with my ex-husband—we do everything we can to prevent our partners from abandoning us. But by compulsively pleasing them while denying our own needs, we abandon ourselves. We end up feeling more alone than if our partner *did* leave us—because nothing outside of us will ever fill the void of our self-abandonment.

> As long as we're abandoning ourselves,
> we will feel alone.

In his book *Love and Awakening: Discovering the Sacred Path of Intimate Relationship*, John Welwood wrote, "As you connect with the feelings that come up when you acknowledge your fear of abandonment, you actually start to heal that abandonment wound, because you're there for yourself in a new way. You're no longer abandoning yourself." Bringing your wounds, beliefs, and shadow selves into consciousness as you've done through the steps in this book is how you heal. It's one of the ways you learn how to show yourself love and take care of your needs first.

It bears repeating: Love is an inside job. No matter how much we wish love could come from external sources, it simply has to start from within. Then, the more we love ourselves, the more love we can accept from others. It's a win-win lovefest all around. And when we love ourselves, we no longer have a port for that "unworthiness cord." In fact, it's only through refusing to abandon ourselves that our relationships with others can flourish.

So this final step is about leaning into loving ourselves first, which will pave the way for leaning into loving someone else and receiving their love in return. Because we can't truly commit to anyone else before we commit to ourselves.

If you're married, you've already made a legal commitment to another person. But you can still recommit to yourself first. Then, you can recommit to staying in your relationship (or not, if you so choose).

Once you've committed to yourself, you'll have the courage and confidence to make choices and take actions that are aligned with *your* truth and desires. And your relationship with the partner of your choice will only be stronger as a result. So let's make your commitment to *you* official.

Exercise #26: Your Self-Love Commitment Contract

Draw up a "Self-Love Commitment Contract" that specifies what you *will* do and what you *won't* do. You can pull from your nonnegotiables, if you like, but you might choose to take it further and get more detailed about your commitment to loving yourself. After you've written your contract, you might also choose to make it more solid by holding a commitment ceremony with friends.

Examples

Here's a full contract from one of my clients (with her name removed):

"I, _____, commit to the following self-love guidelines:

1. *I will take responsibility for my beliefs around what love looks like and feels like.*

2. *I will remember that I'm on equal footing with others.*

3. *I will remember to embrace knowing we're all spiritual brothers and sisters, not competitors.*

4. *I will allow others to be who they are and not feel the need to change them.*

5. *I will embrace my uniqueness and see it as a strength instead of a weakness.*

6. *I will remember to have compassion for my patterns of growth.*

7. *I will remember not to take other people's projections personally.*

8. *I will remember that we all have our own paths and reasons for being.*

9. *I will remember to treat myself with the utmost respect, love, and support.*

10. *I will remember that I'm a divine being first and human being second.*

11. *I will remember to share my heart with those who seek me out for guidance. A success for one is a success for all.*

12. *I won't find excuses and reasons to belittle, judge, criticize, or run myself down.*

13. *I won't feel obligated to put myself in situations I don't want to be in.*

14. *I will express my truth, needs, and desires with honesty, kindness, and grace.*

15. *I will stand my ground when necessary.*

16. *I won't allow my inner perfectionist to run the show of my life. I will give her a nice balcony seat with binoculars for viewing, but she'll no longer have a speaking role! Now she's a bystander. If she shows up unannounced and bossy, I'll simply thank her for appearing and say, 'I was expecting you. The show is about to start, so find a comfortable seat in the veranda section. This next act is called "The Exciting and Unpredictable Adventures of _____." Enjoy the show, but your review will not be heard.'*

17. *Above all, I will remember to thank myself, the angels, guides, and spirit for giving me the best gift I could ever receive—Me!"*

Below are some other "provisions" from my other clients' contracts to give you ideas:

"I commit to the belief that as my genuine self-love grows, the right relationship will arrive."

"I commit to giving myself my own heartfelt attention by spending quality time with myself daily."

"I commit to putting myself first above all others, while still finding ways to be of service that don't sacrifice or deplete me."

"I commit to loving all parts of me, not just the ones I find redeeming."

"I commit to saying 'yes' to the things I desire to do and 'no' to the things I don't, even at the risk of disappointing others. rather than appeasing or pleasing them."

"I commit to letting go of my old victim stories."

"I commit to leaning into love with the best possible partner for me right now."

Now it's your turn! What will you put in your contract? How will you demonstrate your self-love emotionally, physically, and spiritually? When you're finished, print it out and sign it in ink. Post it in your home where you'll see it, if you're comfortable with that, or keep it somewhere handy. Then, refer to it at least once a week to remind you of your commitments. To help you remember, choose a specific time each week when you'll look at it, such as Friday night, Saturday morning, Sunday night, or Monday morning.

HOW DO YOU ACTUALLY LEARN TO LOVE YOURSELF?

All this talk about loving yourself is fine and good. It's a great intellectual exercise, but how do you *actually* do it? While writing this book, I've thought about that question a lot. What I know is that there's no final destination where we love ourselves 100 percent. Like forgiveness, self-love is a practice. We have to remind ourselves of it on a regular basis. We have to recommit to loving ourselves every day.

That said, we do get better at it. When I was married, I didn't have a great deal of self-love available to me. I felt I had to jump through hoops to earn everyone else's love and didn't really think about the need to love myself first. I believed if anyone knew the real me deep inside, they'd withdraw their love. I was so wrong.

Today, my capacity for loving myself is beyond what I could have imagined all those years ago. But there will always be more, and the work of loving myself better will never end.

I got better at loving myself through working with my origin story, limiting beliefs, and underlying commitments—just like you've been doing throughout these chapters. Here are some of the other ways I've learned to love myself more:

Self-talk. While loving ourselves can't be accomplished in the mind—love always has to come from the heart—I've found that the mind can help the heart to open. As we become more aware of what self-love looks like, we can watch for where it is *not* in our lives. For example, I began to realize that I was putting my husband first in virtually every situation, denying myself what I wanted. I believed that if others found out about my failing marriage and my affair, they'd all shun me, leaving me utterly abandoned and alone.

But as I began to see the brutal nature of my perfectionism and its unreasonable demands on me, I also started to recognize that I'm human. I'll always make mistakes, and that's true for everyone. As Louise Hay said to me when I confessed to her that I wasn't perfect, "Did you really think I thought you were the only one who was?" So I got real with myself about the impossibility of perfection.

One of the gateways to leaning into self-love for me was positive self-talk. I told myself that I didn't deserve to be judged so harshly. I could indeed make mistakes and still be lovable.

I began to watch myself each day and ask the question: Am I being self-loving today? Am I putting someone else ahead of me, and if so, why? What do I believe I'll get if I put them before me? What do I believe I'll lose if I don't? Am I talking down to myself?

I noticed that my inner critic would sometimes have a field day with me. *Everybody's going to find out you're a fraud. You were 10 minutes late. How could you do that?* Slowly, but surely, I noticed that voice more and more, and I counteracted it with another voice—a loving voice. This new voice said, *You aren't a fraud, Nancy. Lots of people are late. Ten minutes is nothing. No one is going to care, and if they do, so what? Isn't that their problem?* Over time, my loving voice was louder and more prominent than my inner critic. Be patient with yourself, and try to be content with whatever baby steps you make in this process.

Relax your expectations. Far too often, we attach self-love to expectations. Let's say you apply for a job you really want. If you don't get it, you think less of yourself. Or if your partner says something unkind to you, you're sure it's true and subject yourself to a run of negative self-talk.

Sometimes, I ask myself directly, "If I don't succeed at X or Y, can I still love myself?" "What about if my book is a flop—will I *still* be able to love myself?" If my honest answer is "no," I need to do some work to soften around my expectations.

Remind yourself, too, of all the imperfections you love in other people. Aren't some of their quirks and so-called faults endearing? Wouldn't they be insufferable if they were truly perfect? If we stop thinking of our human foibles as "wrong" or "bad," we can fall in love with our "unfinished" selves as we are right now.

Relinquish worry about what others think. I also began to disengage from worrying about what other people thought of me. I tuned into myself first as you've learned to do in earlier chapters, and I reminded myself that the thoughts of others aren't a reflection of who I am. Their opinions come from their own origin stories, negative beliefs, shadow selves, projections, triggers, and insecurities. That's a lot of stuff to filter through before they reach an opinion about me! It may happen instantaneously, but that's all the more reason why their opinions aren't necessarily valid. They aren't thinking rationally about me; they're reacting automatically.

When we worry about what others think of us and hold on to that childhood belief that our survival depends on their acceptance, we aren't living from our own agency. We're living in reaction to something outside of us. Whenever we try to package ourselves to satisfy someone else, we abandon ourselves. We abandon self-love.

Louise Hay once said to me, "You're the only thinker in your head." That really hit home. No matter what anyone thought of me, it was really what I thought about myself that mattered.

It isn't easy to stop worrying about the opinions of others, but it works if you keep reminding yourself that their opinions are filtered through their own "stuff." Stop right now and imagine what it would feel like to no longer care what others thought of you. What would it be like if no one could criticize or praise you? It isn't easy to imagine, is it? But play with that image. Take a stroll one day this week, pretending you don't care what anyone thinks of you. It doesn't mean you're going to suddenly do something outrageous—unless you want to. It's just a new way of being; try it on for size. How does it feel? If you allow it, not caring can be enormously freeing.

Allow yourself to receive. Another way I opened my heart to myself was allowing myself to receive. This has been a tough one for me. Remember my story about the donut pillow Aaron gave me? I struggle with receiving and take care of my own needs to such a degree that Aaron ends up feeling frustrated because I ask for nothing from him. I'm beginning to understand that by accepting his love, gifts, and assistance, I'm giving him pleasure, in the same way it gives me pleasure to give to someone else from an openhearted (not people-pleasing!) place. When I'm able to share what I've learned in a book like this, for example.

But so many of us have been conditioned to give, give, give—to everyone else instead of ourselves. When someone offers to give you a gift or to help you, do you automatically say, "No, I'm fine," even if you could use the help? Yeah, me too.

Many of us struggle accepting offers from others because we've been told "it's more blessed to give than receive." I understand that sentiment, but if everyone followed it to the letter, who would be left to receive what we give?

Balance can be achieved only if there's a flow of giving and receiving from an open heart to an open heart. The next exercise is a meditation to help you open your heart to receiving more. You'll be able to create a balance that allows you to not only receive from others, but also to receive more of your own self-love.

The strategies you've just read are the ones I've used to lean into loving myself. They all involve day-by-day corrections, often in tiny increments, to your self-critical habits. As you build on those increments, the corrections will become your new habits. Gradually, those new habits will change the way you live. These strategies are what create the port that someone else's healthy love can plug into.

Trust me—I struggled with my self-love efforts at first. I felt as though I was making very little progress. Then, one day, I realized that I put myself first without thinking. I had the loving thought *before* the inner critic started in on me. Then, slowly, self-love became more of a way of being. It became the light that got me out of bed in the morning.

Remember: You're worthy of love just for who you are. Imagine what it would feel like to love yourself unconditionally and know that there's nothing you have to do to earn love. What would that feel like?

That feeling—that experience of being lovable just because you're you—is the goal. The more moments you can feel that, the happier and more peaceful you'll be. That will then translate into more harmonious relationships and more moments when you can extend that unconditional love to others.

But bear in mind that you don't have to be perfect at unconditional love either! Just cultivate as much of it as you can. It's an ideal that none of us can accomplish 24/7. But once in hand, it has the power to transform us like nothing else.

Client Practices for Leaning into Love

Brenda has a terrific practice for leaning into *self-love*. "The most powerful practice for me is to set an intention in the morning to stay present in the relationships I'm most focused on right now," she says. "Then, at the end of the day, I recapitulate, running through a few interactions and checking the quality, as it relates to people-pleasing. High-fives for success are great, but it's more powerful for me to love myself through the moments when old behaviors ruled and evaluate how I might have acted with a do-over."

Charles and his wife have a practice for leaning into loving *each other*. It allows them to show love for each other on a daily basis. Each night when they go to bed, they tell each other three things they appreciate about the other. This practice is especially important to maintain when the energy is tense between them. It reminds them what's still good in the relationship, even when the difficulties are front and center.

Exercise #27: Receiving Love

This final exercise is in two parts. Part 1 is a meditation, and Part 2 involves writing a love letter to yourself.

Part 1—Meditation for Opening the Heart to Receive

In this meditation, you'll open your heart to receiving more love and other wonderful things—first from yourself and then from others. Be sure to turn off all phones so that you can surrender to this process. Wear comfortable clothes, and sit on a comfortable chair or couch. Feel free to play soft music or light candles, if you like. It helps to record your own voice reading the steps so that you don't have to open your eyes, which will disrupt your meditative state. Note that if you are recording your own version, you may want to leave out the italicized portions of the script.

Steps 2 and 3 of the meditation are a repeat from an earlier meditation in which you open to self-love. You can't do this meditation enough. In fact, I suggest you repeat Steps 2 and 3 every day, preferably when you get up in the morning or during your shower.

1. Close your eyes, and take several breaths. Relax each part of your body, starting with your feet. Then, gradually move up your legs, hips, belly, chest, back, arms, neck, and head until you feel fully relaxed. *Don't work too hard at this. Just ask your body to relax. As you continue, it will relax more and more.*

2. Think about the person you most love in the world, someone where the love is uncomplicated and pure. Perhaps a child, a grandparent, or a friend. Feel your heart filling with that love. It might appear as a bright light. Now allow that love to fill your body from the top of your head to the tips of your toes. Allow yourself to take in this love that you feel for the other person.

3. Now turn this love toward yourself. Picture yourself as a young child, maybe as young as two, three, or four years old. See the little one you were flooded with love. Give as much of this love to yourself as you can, knowing that you're still this young child deep within. Know that you deserve this love just as much as the other person you love so deeply.

4. Now picture your heart in your mind's eye or feel its presence. (I'm referring here to your energetic heart rather than the actual organ.) Imagine that your heart is blooming like a flower, and as the petals open wider and wider, space is being made for you to receive. Allow the love you just filled yourself with to penetrate your heart, filling it until it overflows.

5. Next, allow love to come to you from wherever it wants. You may feel it as light

or rose petals being showered on you. Have fun with it! Let it be whatever feels really good to you.

6. Then, repeat either aloud or in your mind, "I welcome more goodness, beauty, and happiness to come to me. I'll look for opportunities to accept love in whatever form it comes. It might be a gift, a compliment, a smile, a gesture, a hug. I affirm that I'll take this love because I deserve it and because I love myself enough to receive it with gratitude."

7. Then, when you're ready, open your eyes and take a deep breath. *You can't do this meditation too much! Whenever you've had a rough day, or your self-loving has taken a beating, come back to this meditation. If you're feeling down on yourself, it may be more difficult to do, but that's exactly when you need it most! So even if you can only feel it a little, it will help you to open your heart more to yourself.*

Part 2—Love Letter to Yourself

In keeping with our discussion of unconditional love, in this exercise, you'll write a love letter to yourself. Unlike the self-love commitment contract, which is about your future commitments to yourself, this is a letter of love and appreciation for yourself exactly as you are right now at this moment. If you've done this before, please do it again. Your capacity for self-love will be deeper after reading this book.

If you find this exercise difficult, write the letter to your inner child instead of the adult version of you. Seeing the young, innocent version of you may make it easier.

When you're finished with your letter, try this: Give it to a trustworthy friend, and ask him/her to send it to you in six months. Or tape it above your door with a date after which you'll take it down and read it again. When you read it after some time has passed, note if you can feel that your self-love increased since you wrote the letter. If not, don't beat yourself up! Simply commit to trying the strategies in this chapter and/or working with some of the other exercises in the book.

Below are three love letter examples from my clients to help you get started:

"Dear Me,

"As I gaze upon who you are at this very moment, I stand in awe of the love that you hold in your heart. The way you treat your beloveds and strangers alike. The curiosity you have developed about life. Your passion for all things mystical. The way you move through the world has become a beautiful dance to witness and be a part of creating. I hope you will give yourself moments of awe where you just sit and know the deep well of love that you are! I love you. I see you."

"Dear Mindful One,

"WOW! I'm so honored to see the person you have become in the past few years. The work you've done to resolve relationships, both with yourself and others, continues to inspire. While this hasn't been an easy process in any respect, you've taken on the hard and easy work with the same level of commitment to ensure growth and cleansing. Finding the ability to love yourself has opened you to better love others. I think you'll agree that the person you were even a few months ago is simply a ghost of who you are now. I'm excited to see how each day can potentially bring a 'new' marriage to your marriage. Allow me to give you a big hug. I truly love who you have become and continue to grow into.

"Love, Charles"

"Dear sweet baby girl, creative enchantress, divine goddess, beautiful soul,

"I acknowledge you for the work you've done and are doing. It's hard work, and I'm proud of you. You've come a long way. I believe you'll create the abundant life you desire. But it must have been painful to feel unsafe and afraid that someone might hurt you. Especially when it came from the people who loved you the most. I'm so sorry you had to hear that, feel that, run away, and hide. I'm so sorry that you took it all into your heart and your body. I wish I could have been there to hold you when you were hiding. I wish I could have told you that it was good to cry and scream and cuss and beat your fists on the cold ground sometimes. I understand this is why you stopped singing. But it's okay now. This is the time to love every bit of yourself. It's time to love and cherish each moment, every sentiment, and every test that brought you to this gorgeous moment. All of the judgments, joys, scars, hidden tears, screams, and fears are a part of this wonderful and enchanted woman you've become. You are loved, so loved, my beloved child, my extraordinary, magnificent woman. It's time to sing again and be heard."

FALL IN LOVE WITH YOURSELF

The time has come, my beloveds. You have the new relationship blueprint in your hands. You see that having a relationship is really signing up for school. You know that the most important love affair you will ever have in this lifetime is with yourself. You know that the only thing you need to feel desperate about is whether you are loving yourself, caring for yourself, and putting yourself first. (If you still feel "desperate" about finding a relationship, now's the time to go back and redo Step 1. Some part of you needed to make it through the whole process in order to go back and take the first step—and that's beautiful and you can trust it.)

My Wish for You

My wish for you is that the seed of self-love, awakened within these pages, will bloom big—beyond what you can even imagine. That your love of self will bring wholeness, and the love of another will bring healing.

My wish for you is that *boundaries* will no longer be a dirty word. You'll know they're simply the limits you set around what you will and will not do, as well as what you will and will not accept or tolerate from others. And that you'll remember these boundaries are yours to uphold.

My wish for you is that you will ask yourself these questions each day: What's the most self-honoring choice I can make today? What's the most self-loving action I can take today? And then, you'll make that choice and take that action.

My wish for you is that you will fall in love with yourself first—knowing that it's only when you finally give permission to all parts of yourself to be present, and love them in their fullness, that you'll be available for the love you desire.

loving and being loved

sometimes
i still find it
so confronting to listen
closely for my desire
as it rises
still so easy for it
to be blocked out by
what someone else needs

we who are used to
abandoning ourselves
for the sake of another
or avoiding feeling
by any sort of
sublimation
it takes longer to listen
to the voice inside
reminding us
that it's only when we finally
honor all parts of ourselves
with permission to attend to
our fullness
that we will be available
for mindful union

i know we all want
to be heard seen felt met
yet in conflict
may we remember
that staying in connection
is most important

sometimes
i believe
loving in disconnection
is truly the most sacred
practice

as myth moves out of us
we have truly underestimated
who we are

lifetimes return
passion engages
heartbeats between blooms
in the shadow of caress

the mountains whisper
while embracing
another year

and all the time
i am certain
that self-love
is at the root
nourishing my heart
to meet yours

i am being called
to stand my ground
while loving
and being loved

relationship is a
recurring rhythm
sovereign
inside another

intimacy
inscribed on the heart
i belong

♥

Resources

Personality Assessments

The Enneagram Institute: www.enneagraminstitute.com

The 5 Love Languages, Gary Chapman: www.5lovelanguages.com

The Myers & Briggs Foundation: www.myersbriggs.org

Stan Tatkin, founder of the PACT Method (Psychobiological Approach to Couple Therapy®): www.stantatkin.com

Integrative Coaching Certification

The Ford Institute for Transformational Training: www.thefordinstitute.com

If you are in an abusive relationship:

The National Domestic Violence Hotline: www.thehotline.org, 1-800-799-7233

Acknowledgments

Deep bows of gratitude for the limitless love and support of so many.

Louise Hay: For being the beginning. I miss you.

Reid Tracy: For seeing me, believing in me, encouraging me, celebrating me.

Debbie Ford: For the great honor of carrying your legacy forward.

Melanie Votaw: For your devotion to bringing my heart and voice alive on the page with grace, depth, precision, and radiance. I have learned much with you about collaboration, a foundation of this book, and don't ever want to write a book without you!

Pat Denzer, Tracy Phillips, Danita Currie, Ayesha Ophelia, Petra Boucher, Terry Nolan: For being my phenomenal team behind the scenes. I appreciate each one of you and all you do so very much.

Lean Into Love-ers: For my trusted tribe of clients with whom I first shared this work, a zillion thank-yous for allowing me to guide you through this process as it was still taking shape, for all the stories and pieces of yourself you shared within these pages, and for the impact each one of you has had on me.

My Coaching Clients: For trusting me to guide and witness you.

Julie Stroud (my secret weapon), Kelley Kosow, and the Ford Institute: For your continued support and for being family.

My Hay House Family: There are far too many of you to name, but I *must* name with thanks and love: Margarete Nielsen, Mollie Langer, Christa Gabler, Matt Wood,

Adrian Sandoval, Anne Barthel, Michelle Pilley, Diane Hill, Richelle Fredson.

Steve Morris, Mike Joseph, Rocky George, and the whole Hay House Radio crew: Thank you for making *Jump Start Your Life* such a joy each week and helping me shine.

Gabby Bernstein, Kris Carr, Barbara Carrellas, Ahlea Khadro, Maya Labos, Christiane Northrup, Kate Northrup, Nick Ortner, Daniel Peralta, Linda Perry, Sallie Ward Robinson: For the singular and significant support you've provided as I rise.

Colette Baron-Reid: For trusting me.

Raven Wells: For holding us capable of loving ourselves and each other as you expertly navigate the uncharted with us.

Melissa Grace: For embracing and loving the fullness of me.

Patty Gift: For gracing this book with your ace edit; and for your effortless companionship as we roam around theatering, dining, and sharing sacred moments.

Kelly Notaras: For your unparalleled heart and being the other half of us. You will forever be my NSLP.

Mom and Dad: For life and love, which is everything.

Kate Aks: For being the other half of my heartbeat . . . and for sharing Allan, Isabel, and Simon with me.

Aaron Thomas: For your passionate spirit of curiosity, adventure, and pleasure-seeking (that I sometimes fight tooth and nail); for your willingness and openness on our healing journey of love (even when it's a challenge); for learning about intimacy, trust, communication, and collaboration side by side; and for (this is a *big* one) taking care of me. Who I am today wouldn't be possible without you to rub up against (figuratively and literally). I love you and am grateful for each day with you.

ABOUT THE AUTHOR

Nancy Levin is the bestselling author of *Worthy, Jump... And Your Life Will Appear* and *Writing for My Life*. She is a Master Integrative Coach and the creator of several in-depth coaching programmes, guiding clients to live life on their own terms and make themselves a priority. She was the Event Director at Hay House from 2002–2014 and hosts her own weekly call-in show, *Jump Start Your Life*, on Hay House Radio. Nancy received her MFA in Creative Writing and Poetics from Naropa University in Boulder, Colorado, and she continues to live in the Rocky Mountains.

www.nancylevin.com

INTRODUCTION

As the Event Director at the book publisher Hay House for over a decade, I was known as the person who could achieve the impossible. One particular feat illustrates what I mean. I was producing two back-to-back live events with best-selling author Dr. Wayne Dyer over a single weekend. He spoke in Atlanta on Saturday afternoon. Then, we flew to Detroit for a Sunday afternoon event.

Late Saturday evening, a panicked Wayne called me in my hotel room in Detroit. "I can't find my briefcase! I'm sure I left it somewhere en route from Atlanta." Everything he needed for his lecture was in that briefcase, and he was convinced he wouldn't be able to take the stage without it.

The over-giving Superwoman that I was kicked into high gear. I remembered he had his briefcase in the van to the airport in Atlanta, so I called the car company. At first, they said they couldn't find it, but I begged them to check again. On the second look, they found it hiding under a seat—but it was almost midnight by then.

I called Wayne. "Go to bed, and don't worry. I'll figure out some way to get your briefcase to you in time."

I asked the car company to put an employee on a plane to Detroit, and they said they could not do that. My efforts to find a delivery service failed; after all, it was midnight on Saturday night.

I didn't sleep. At 4 A.M., I jumped into a taxi and used my laptop to buy the first available round-trip plane ticket to Atlanta. When I landed, I ran outside to meet the driver from the car company at baggage claim. Briefcase in hand, I went back through security to catch the flight back to Detroit. TSA stopped me and questioned me profusely. Why was I was traveling with only a briefcase? Why I was I flying straight back to the city I had just arrived from? I must have looked pretty suspicious. Who flies round-trip just to pick up a briefcase?

Wayne was just waking up as I boarded the plane back to Detroit. I called him before we took off and told him I had his briefcase.

"Nancy, did you do something crazy?"

I managed to get to the event venue in Detroit just minutes before Wayne's car arrived. Ta-da! I could still claim my moniker of Superwoman. I was so relieved.

Acts of heroism like this one were normal for me back then. Just another example of how I went to "crazy" lengths, as Wayne put it, to make sure I earned gold stars from everyone in my life. In the process—almost always—I paid no attention to what I needed for myself. I constantly allowed my own boundaries to be crossed . . . and crossed . . . and crossed again.

This was especially true in my marriage. But when you deny your own needs for so many years, eventually they simply refuse to be denied any longer. They end up getting expressed "sideways." For me, that expression was an affair—a sideways assertion of my needs in response to my constant refusal to set boundaries.

It took eight years after the affair was over for the reckoning to happen—the one that would blow up my life. It arrived in the form of a voice mail from my husband as I sat in the San Diego airport, waiting for a plane to take me home to Colorado. "I read your journals. You'd better get your ass home—there's hell to pay."

I had a full 70 journals. Could he have possibly read "that one"? The one in which I wrote about the affair from eight years earlier?

The flight home was a blur. It felt like I was on my way to my execution.

When I got home, my husband was just inside the door, holding four of my journals. "I'm going to make copies of some of these pages and send them to everybody you know, including your parents and co-workers. I look forward to seeing what they think once they know the *real* you."

The real me. I had spent years hiding the real me. I worked hard to design a life that had *no room* for me. At that time, the idea that people could truly know me in all my vulnerabilities was nothing short of terror-inducing. I was sure, as my husband seemed to be saying, that I'd become an outcast as soon as they knew "the truth."

I was so afraid of anyone discovering my humanity that I was a champion "do-it-all doormat." I believed the only way I could be loved was by presenting my façade of Superwoman to everyone in my life, from my family, to my friends, to my co-workers. I had to be the person everyone needed me to be— the chameleon who would put her own needs aside to make sure everyone else's needs were met. Who was I truly, and what did I need for myself? That question wasn't even on my map.

Not only did I fail to set boundaries, but I never even *dreamed of* setting them. Doing so would risk making someone else unhappy. To my mind, that was a risk I couldn't afford to take.

So after my husband threatened to tell everyone what he discovered in my journals, I still tried to make our marriage work. Ten months after that awful night, he kicked me out of the house. (The house I had bought and paid for, by the way.) Oh, and it was my birthday.

I returned and tried again. And again. And again. And again. The fifth time he threw me out was January 12, 2010, and that was when I finally put the "do-it-all doormat" on notice that she was no longer going to run my life. That fifth time, I finally asserted a boundary . . . by not going back.

That was the beginning of my quest to become a boundary badass. But it meant I had to stop saying yes to others' needs, wants, and desires in order to be loved and accepted. It meant I had to learn how to tell the truth and create connection with others in a more authentic way, rather than by wowing them with one selfless act after the next. It was a difficult transition, with lots of ups and downs. But I'm happy to report that the journey was well worth it. Following this path would lead to a kind of freedom I never knew existed—a freedom that has changed the course of my life forever.

What Is a Boundary?

A boundary is, in essence, where you end, and another person begins. I define it as a limit that you set to define what you will and will not do, or what you will or will not accept or tolerate from others. (Throughout the book I will also use the word "limit" as a synonym for "boundary.") Boundaries are completely natural and automatic. When the body hits its limit, we feel physical pain. When the heart or emotional system hits its limit, we feel anger, sadness, or hurt. These boundaries come preloaded into the human experience. Sometimes we can train ourselves to push past our natural limits—like the time I ran a 17-mile race over a 13,000-foot mountain pass . . . ouch! But there's no way to get rid of boundaries entirely.

So how do you know where your natural ones lie? You must be able to feel them, both physically and emotionally. When experiences feel decidedly positive, you're in the green zone. No boundaries nearby. When they feel neutral, or a little shaky— like you're not sure whether this is good or bad—you're in the yellow zone. A boundary is probably a few steps away. Then, of course, there are experiences that clearly feel bad. We experience pain—physical, mental, or emotional. When "neutral" experience gives way to "negative" experience, you know you're in the red zone, and a boundary has already been crossed.

Our emotional and physical systems are tracking our boundaries all the time. The trouble—the reason I'm writing this book at all—is that in many cases, our conscious mind is totally unaware we have a boundary, much less that it's been crossed. For lots of reasons that I will talk about in detail throughout the book, we have learned to suppress from our mind's awareness enormous amounts of information that are being registered at the level of the heart and gut—information about our limits and when they've been reached.

The result of this "boundary blindness" is that our natural boundaries are frequently getting crossed—and most of the time, we don't even know it's happening. Ever feel angry, resentful, shut down, or helpless? These are good warning signs that something is off. You've gone past your limit, and you're in the red zone. It's time to retrace your steps back to the place where you felt good, safe, and happy. The dividing line between positive and negative experience is a natural boundary that somehow got crossed.

Now you may be asking, "Negative experience *always* signals a boundary has been crossed? Isn't negative experience a part of life?" The answer to both questions is the same: Yes. Negative experience signals a boundary has been crossed. And yes, negative experiences are part of being human. Having our limits exceeded from time to time in our lives is inevitable. We will lose people we love, get into fender benders, stub our toes and howl in pain. Nobody would choose *these* experiences, and often they are out of our control.

This doesn't mean we're powerless to create a life that is better and better with each day that passes, however. Too often, I meet clients who have relinquished the boundaries over which they *do* have control, calling them inevitable when they are not.

That is what this book is about. Leaving the boundary-crossing acts of god to the side, we will be doing a deep dive with the ordinary, daily boundary crossings that we've been choosing to keep in place. The violations of our space, time, physical, and emotional comfort that we are allowing (consciously or unconsciously) every day.

So how do we "set a boundary"? We do it by naming the limits that already exist. We're not making up something new; we're just putting into words the needs and wants that have been there all along, under the surface. In this way, we make the unconscious conscious. We tell ourselves (and others) that certain experiences will not be tolerated, because they are not healthy for us and don't feel good. Locating and declaring our boundaries allows us to take care of our own needs—physical, emotional, energetic, mental, and material.

We all have many different types of boundaries. Here are a few obvious ones:

Physical boundaries pertain to your body, your personal space, your time, and your privacy. For example, if someone touches you in a way that makes you feel uncomfortable, they have crossed your physical boundary—even if that was not their intention.

Emotional boundaries pertain to your emotional needs—and the needs of others. For example, you might not want to stand by and watch while your mother berates your father.

Mental boundaries pertain to your thoughts, values, and opinions. An example might be listening to someone go on a misogynistic rant. You don't like what's being said—it feels terrible to you—and as such, your mental boundary is being crossed.

Material boundaries pertain to money and property that belong to you. For example, you may feel a contraction when your friends suggest splitting the dinner bill evenly, even though everyone else at the table shared a bottle of wine and you were not drinking.

Our boundaries are all about who we are and what *we* want and need. Boundaries help us feel our best and make it possible for us to live the life we most desire. If you want to experience more joy and excitement in your life, it all begins with boundaries.

Hay House Titles of Related Interest

YOU CAN HEAL YOUR LIFE, the movie,
starring Louise Hay & Friends
(available as a 1-DVD program, an expanded 2-DVD set,
and an online streaming video)
Learn more at www.hayhouse.com/louise-movie

THE SHIFT, the movie,
starring Dr. Wayne W. Dyer
(available as a 1-DVD program, an expanded 2-DVD set,
and an online streaming video)
Learn more at www.hayhouse.com/the-shift-movie

* * *

*CONSCIOUS LOVING EVER AFTER: How to Create
Thriving Relationships at Midlife and Beyond,*
by Gay Hendricks, Ph.D., and Kathlyn Hendricks, Ph.D.

*DODGING ENERGY VAMPIRES: An Empath's Guide to
Evading Relationships That Drain You and Restoring
Your Health and Power,* by Christiane Northrup, M.D.

*QUANTUM LOVE: Use Your Body's Atomic Energy to Create the
Relationship You Desire,* by Laura Berman, Ph.D.

UNLOCKING SECRETS: My Journey to an Open Heart,
by Kathe Crawford

All of the above are available at www.hayhouse.co.uk.

* * *

Hay House Podcasts
Bring Fresh, Free Inspiration Each Week!

Hay House proudly offers a selection of life-changing
audio content via our most popular podcasts!

Hay House Meditations Podcast

Features your favorite Hay House authors guiding you through meditations designed to help you relax and rejuvenate. Take their words
into your soul and cruise through the week!

Dr. Wayne W. Dyer Podcast

Discover the timeless wisdom of Dr. Wayne W. Dyer, world-renowned
spiritual teacher and affectionately known as "the father of motivation." Each week brings some of the best selections from the 10-year
span of Dr. Dyer's talk show on HayHouseRadio.com.

Hay House World Summit Podcast

Over 1 million people from 217 countries and territories participate in
the massive online event known as the Hay House World Summit. This
podcast offers weekly mini-lessons from World Summits past as a taste
of what you can hear during the annual event, which occurs each May.

Hay House Radio Podcast

Listen to some of the best moments from HayHouseRadio.com,
featuring expert authors such as Dr. Christiane Northrup, Anthony
William, Caroline Myss, James Van Praagh, and Doreen Virtue
discussing topics such as health, self-healing, motivation, spirituality,
positive psychology, and personal development.

Hay House Live Podcast

Enjoy a selection of insightful and inspiring lectures from Hay House Live,
an exciting event series that features Hay House authors and leading
experts in the fields of alternative health, nutrition, intuitive medicine,
success, and more! Feel the electricity of our authors engaging with a
live audience, and get motivated to live your best life possible!

Find Hay House podcasts on iTunes, or visit
www.HayHouse.com/podcasts for more info.

HAY HOUSE

Look within

Join the conversation about latest products,
events, exclusive offers and more.

 Hay House UK

 @HayHouseUK

 @hayhouseuk

 healyourlife.com

We'd love to hear from you!